The Blue
in the Air

The Blue
in the Air

Marcello Carlin

Winchester, UK
Washington, USA

First published by Zero Books, 2011
Zero Books is an imprint of John Hunt Publishing Ltd., The Bothy, Deershot Lodge, Park Lane,
Ropley, Hants, SO24 0BE, UK
office1@o-books.net
www.o-books.com

For distributor details and how to order please visit the 'Ordering' section on our website.

Text copyright: Marcello Carlin 2010

ISBN: 978 1 84694 596 0

A CIP catalogue record for this book is available from the British Library.

Design: Stuart Davies

Printed in the UK by CPI Antony Rowe
Printed in the USA by Offset Paperback Mfrs, Inc

We operate a distinctive and ethical publishing philosophy in all
areas of our business, from our global network of authors to
production and worldwide distribution.

CONTENTS

Introduction

Most music writers write for a living, but I began writing about music in order to live. My first partner, Laura Gerrard, died of cancer in August 2001 at the age of thirty-six. That the ensuing period was not a happy time for me scarcely needs to be said, and for most of it the last thing I wanted to do was to listen to music. Still, it quickly became apparent that this was no route back towards any life worthy of the name, and that to survive, let alone come to terms with my own grief, would involve coming to terms with music, not simply the music that Laura and I had shared for many, many years, but all the music that Laura would now be unable to hear. I felt I owed it to her memory, not only to pay due tribute to her spirit, but also to do all the new listening for her. If I could do this in public, moreover, then perhaps other spirits would stumble upon me, and even connect with me.

With some considerable encouragement from others, I felt confident enough to want to approach both writing and music again, and *The Church Of Me*, named after the planned but unbuilt memorial to the first wife of the artist Stanley Spencer, stumbled into existence at the beginning of 2002. The blog became quickly and surprisingly popular, perhaps because there were few other websites at the time devoted to long-form analytical music writing, and fewer still with such unavoidable personal content. Certainly the latter, together with the perceived quality of the writing, struck a chord with many readers as well as other bloggers. One Toronto-based blogger, Lena Friesen, thought enough of *The Church Of Me* to want to get in touch with its writer and so, in 2003, what effectively began as an online penpal relationship slowly developed over the next couple of years into something more profound. We met, became engaged, married – in Toronto – in November 2007, and little over a year later she finally came to join me permanently in London. While awaiting her arrival I began a new blog – *The Blue In The Air*. Although this blog had no overt agenda, I found that, in retrospect, the posts did tell an accidentally profound story. While I was waiting patiently for my world to change forever and for the better, the world too seemed to be waiting for change; this period covered Barack Obama's nomination for the Democratic presidential candidacy and eventual election as President. Despite the well-documented economic collapse which occurred towards the latter half of 2008, there did appear to be a definite air of optimism, and I hope that this feeling is palpable in the pieces which I have selected for the present collection. Indeed the sense of optimism, although cautious and mindful of wider global crises, has pervaded into the change in British politics which is currently being undertaken as I write these words.

Of the more than two hundred posts which I made over this period to *The Blue In The Air* – read Joan Didion's novel *Democracy* and discover the idea which inspired the title – I decided to select fifty, the half-century which collectively told the best story. I have also included the dates of their original postings in order to contextualize my situation at the time. The pieces here are not always the blog's most celebrated works; my eleven-part essay on Portishead's *Third* album, for example, is omitted as it is really a separate work which does not advance the underlying story. I have taken caution to keep the number of pieces about then-contemporary songs to a relative minimum; time and perspective may yet change my feelings about many of these.

Although this volume does include some essays on well-known songs and performances, I have largely concentrated on those songs which have tended to become overlooked, or even lost, despite an age where any piece of music, however obscure, can be located somewhere on the internet. The unhelpful narrowcast canonization of "classics" persists, with the result that whole movements of music have become muddled, opaque in listeners' awareness or perception of them. Much of what is written about here has become forgotten, or misunderstood, or simply never heard (of) in the first place, and it is my hope – as it should be of any music writer worth their salt – that readers will be inspired by these observations to investigate the songs under consideration, and more besides.

A cursory reading of the book will reveal that these pieces take in an extremely broad range of musical experience, from Britney Spears to Karlheinz Stockhausen. Some may wonder about the elasticity of definition of the term "song"; indeed, one of the "songs" written about is an hour-long piece of radio drama from the 1930s, although music plays a vital part in its development, and its performance and arrangement are in themselves as musical as anything Honegger or Britten were composing at the time. I ascribe this to the joint influences of my parents – my late father, who was passionate about contemporary music of all kinds but especially post-Parker jazz, improvised music, and post-Darmstadt classical, and my mother, who continues to be a fervent fan of pop music of all stripes. It is to be hoped, however, that the revolutions instigated by the internet, particularly the ability to access virtually all music at random, will include a regeneration of eclectic interests and passions on the part of music lovers, to defy easy, profitable demographic categorisation, and this volume may go a little way towards that enviable horizon.

The tone of the various pieces varies in accordance with the feelings inspired by the songs at the time of their writing. All of these pieces were written relatively quickly – on the turn of the proverbial dime – and I have resisted the temptation to update the content or revise my opinions with the benefit of hindsight. I have broadened the original writing out somewhat, since the assumption of shared knowledge when one is writing for a blog with a known and knowing readership cannot be transferred to a published volume aimed at a wider market. The meditation on Jay-Z's performance at Glastonbury 2008 seems to me the pivotal piece, the marker of the point where everything did change, not just for myself but also for the world. In contrast to the considered tone of much of the other writing here, the Jay-Z piece is one of several attempts at ekphrasis – a work of art inspired by another work of a different art – but approaches from casual to formal can all be found within this book, hopefully all written in the same identifiable voice.

Thanks are due to Tariq Goddard at Zer0 Books, who approached me with the original idea for this book at a time when I was expecting no approaches whatsoever, and to Matthew Ingram for making him aware of my existence, as well as to Mark Fisher and John Hunt for their immense help and encouragement with regard to this project. Wise words, corrections and diversions were, as always, offered, or at any rate suggested, by Mark Sinker. I also thank Ian Penman for his invaluable links. On a less personal level I am indebted to Max Harrison, David Thomson, Roger Lewis and Simon Barnes, writers in different fields who have taught me by example never to jump to the obvious conclusion, but equally never to be perverse for perversity's sake. Above all I offer limitless love and gratitude to my dear wife Lena Friesen, without whom this book could have been neither imagined nor written.

Marcello Carlin
London SW6
May 2010

1

Marty Wilde: Abergavenny

17 September 2007

The *sui generis* Sir Cliff Richard being automatically discounted, Marty Wilde has to qualify as the most durable and consistently adventurous survivor of the first Britpop boom of the late fifties – and as an active songwriter and producer as well as a singer, may well outdo Cliff. In the early seventies, while the latter was occupied making God-pestering anthems for the Festival of Light, Wilde was heroically attempting to hitch a ride in the glam carriage under the pseudonym of Zappo before turning his attention to writing for and producing son Ricky and his extraordinary, if brief, run of squalling teen anthems on the UK label (most notably 1974's gloriously cacophonic "Teen Wave") – and then of course his elder daughter Kim grew up, and both father and son collaborated in creating that exceptional run of meta-hits, so spellbinding that you could almost believe that a place called "East California" existed.

Getting there, however, was a struggle. Cliff apart, all of the fifties idols suffered to a greater and lesser extent in the wake of the Beatles, and Wilde, more than most, faced the inevitable prejudices; even though he grew both hair and beard to form the Wilde Three, giving Justin Hayward his first break, he was still seen as the winsome contralto of a spent era. Undeterred, he developed his songwriting skills and enjoyed his first annus mirabilis in 1968 when, writing under the pseudonym of "Frere Manston" in collaboration with one "Jack Gellar," the real name of Ronnie Scott (a different Ronnie Scott from the late saxophonist and club owner), he scored three top ten hits – the

Mersey-flowing-into-sunshine pop balladry of the Casuals' "Jesamine," Lulu's "I'm A Tiger" (about which Ms Lawrie felt much the same as she did about "Boom-Bang-A-Bang") and Status Quo's "Ice In The Sun."

Both the Casuals and Quo records suggest a light dripping of post-psychedelia with rich, unexpected chord changes, and much of this also flows into "Abergavenny". Released under Wilde's own name as a single in 1968 it received considerable radio play in the UK but failed to chart; undeterred, Wilde issued the single in America the following year under the alias of "Shannon" (and no, he was nothing to do with the Shannon responsible for "Let The Music Play," "Give Me Tonight," etc., though wouldn't it have been nice if he had been?); it was a fairly big hit in the States and a major hit in Canada, a welcome but surprising achievement considering its inherent Britishness. From its opening fife and drums fanfare to its brooding intro of wobbly fuzztone guitar with acoustic backing, "Abergavenny" is benign bubblegum with indistinct shadows. Wilde sounds cheerful and eager about "Taking a trip (now there's a clue) up to Abergavenny/Hoping the weather is fine" before drums and bass enter and the pace accelerates: "If you should see a red dog running free/Then you know it's mine," followed by an ecstatically descending piano mimicking said dog gleefully trotting downhill before landing squarely on the 4/4 beat. "I've got to get there and fast," sings Wilde as though the real world is too grey to delay his "trip," before offering a wink to the listener, or perhaps the square: "If you can't go" – with an exaggerated Terry-Thomas emphasis on the sustained "o" of that "go" – "then I promise to show you a photograph." In other words, you have to experience the "trip" in person; as an indirect witness it can only make sense to a certain extent.

As strings caress the lower ground of the middle eight, Wilde offers his extremely 1968 musings about "paradise people" (who are "fine by me") before his own voice drifts in and out of fuzzy warp as he licks the ice cream concept of "Sunshine forever/Lovely weather" before raising an eyebrow – "Don't you wish you could beeeeeee..../TAKING a TRIP up to Abergavenny?" In order to release the escalating tension he gives his best Butlins redcoat prompt of "Everybody now!" as a brass band (plus marching band glockenspiel) parps its way into the song; not quite a summer village fete but also not quite the bierkeller pop which its pedigree might initially suggest, and by "bierkeller pop" I'm thinking of things like Chris Andrews' "To Whom It Concerns" (the instrumental backing track of which became much better known as the theme to Irish television's *The Late, Late Show*) and the Dave Clark Five's "Red Balloon" – a genre which subsequently flourished only in Eurovision and the later hits of Peters and Lee.

A much more relevant source of inspiration may well have been Jack Nitzsche's stoned charts for the Turtles' "She'd Rather Be With Me" – a number four hit at the height of the British Summer of Love – and as a British (or English, even though the subject matter is Welsh) equivalent "Abergavenny" sparkles with marveling effervescence. The record climaxes with celebratory unisons and subtle dislocation, Wilde still mocking the Old Guard with his "A leetle photo-GRAPH!" as the parade passes out of earshot towards their own nirvana, Wilde's closing "la la" cries sounding not that far removed from Francis Rossi. Reissued on CD only recently, after being absent from British circulation for nearly forty years, listening to it conjured up my 1968 with unimaginable rapidity ... and it is easy to discern how such a mischievous spirit in music could go on to be responsible for "Chequered Love" - certainly the journey from "Abergavenny" to "Cambodia" is one of the most remarkable of any pop star of his generation. Including Cliff's.

2

Marcel King: Reach For Love

18 September 2007

Ten years previously he had been at number one as the 16-year-old lead singer of Manchester soul octet Sweet Sensation, made famous by the British television talent show *New Faces*, with "Sad Sweet Dreamer". The last Tony Hatch production to date to top the UK charts, the record indeed blends sadness and sweetness in a way that is uniquely British; King sings the song with a passion almost uncomfortable for a would-be child star, even a Moss Side Michael Jackson, against the swirling strings and palais band saxophones which unmistakably nail the single as Pye Records in 1974, with that very characteristic Marble Arch studio echo.

But the fame did not last; after one more hit, the band struggled despite many fine singles (especially "Hide Away From The Sun") and after a failed attempt to gain the British nomination for 1977 Eurovision split up. What became of Marcel King in the intervening years is unclear, but in the spring of 1984 he abruptly and unexpectedly re-emerged on Factory Records with the one-off single "Reach For Love" (FAC 92). Produced by Bernard Sumner, it received enthusiastic, if slightly baffled, notices in the music press but sold minimally, even though it filled the floor of the Haçienda regularly; to this day Shaun Ryder regards it as the best record Factory ever released. King more or less vanished again until his death in 1995 from a brain haemorrhage, aged just 38. Two years later his son Zeus was shot dead in a drug feud; he was nineteen.

Superficially, then, here we have another story of a child

prodigy who didn't, or wasn't allowed to, fulfill his promise. I am sure the full tale is a lot more complex and less able to fit into preordained storylines. But listening to "Reach For Love" now, it seems like a pop single just slightly out of its time – it should have been a huge hit, but Factory's legendarily crap distribution and marketing facilities militated against that, as did lack of radio play. There is also the question of whether "Reach For Love" was slightly too intense a song and performance to become that huge a hit. The rhythm and bass lines set up at the beginning thrust themselves forward in a somewhat menacing manner, although their propulsion cannot be denied; Happy Mondays would go on to use it as their 1988-9 rhythmic template. The beats are intense enough to qualify as rock rather than dance; there is an unusual thickness to their solidity.

When King's voice first enters – "Girl when I first met you" – we could almost be listening to a better Bros, but he then develops a seamless union between grace (the floating stream of "so strong" in the line "Our love was so strong") and franticity (the teeth-extracting agony of "feel" in "Now I feel everything's going wrong," echoed by the emergence of a high-pitched string synth). Then the track lightens for ripples of sunlit electronics to decorate the chorus of "Everybody needs love baby/Ain't no lying/Everybody wants love babe/We've got to keep on...striving!" and suddenly we are in 1990 Madchester half a decade early.

King continues to extemporize on his increasing pain – "I've been trying to show you better things," he exclaims while an icy backing chorus chants "You keep on giving me shots!" (make whatever analogy you will of that) – climaxing in the bloodcurdling "freeeeeeeeeeeze" of "I freeze, baby, at the thought of leaving you behind." This is vocal control of an exceptionally high level, both technically and emotionally. As the string synths melt into formalism behind him he is preaching to the grey skies: "Girl when you reach for love you've got to hold onto it!/Music is the love that helps me through **EVERYTHING**...makes you hold on, move on..." and his perspective shifts from the girl to music as salvation ("Yes it does," he whimpers, "Sweet music," the backing chorus responds). As a dance record it is exceptionally forceful, perhaps too forceful for the general treble-friendly politesse of 1984 daytime radio; and it only ever appeared as a twelve-inch single, clocking in at just under five and a half minutes. Overall, however, there was something just too real about "Reach For Love" for it to thrive in a culture of masks, irony and timidity. Yet it now stands as one of the great pop hits that never was (or hasn't yet been) and should be sought out and cherished to demonstrate the untapped greatness of this saddest and sweetest of dreamers.

3

Kevin Rowland: This Guy's In Love With You

19 September 2007

This isn't one of the big setpieces on that psychotherapeutic tool of a covers album *My Beauty* but it is one of the most emotionally naked of its tracks, even on a record which set new standards for emotional nakedness. "This Guy's In Love" is another song which interpreters have to approach with extreme caution; it is easy to convert vulnerable into bland, or collapse through the trapdoor of overkill on the key line of "if not I'll just die." Originally composed with Chet Baker in mind – although the Chet Baker of 1968 was in no condition to tackle it – Alpert's voice preserves Baker's pretend nonchalance to conceal his extreme fear and uncertainty; humming to himself in the park, hands insecurely hunched in pockets, while swerving his head around every two seconds to ensure that she's heard him. Rowland's reading, as with much else on *My Beauty*, puts me in mind of Robin Williams' character in *The Fisher King*; his life having been razed to ground zero, clumsily and fitfully but faithfully attempting to build a new one, needing to relearn just about everything in terms of what a human being is and how that human being relates to other ones ("After being so lost and seeing only ugliness in the world, these songs started to penetrate my frightened world" remarks Rowland in his brief sleevenote ... well, that's why some of us build *Churches* ...). He keeps the song very quiet indeed, as a sort of midnight blue jazz ballad, though this is as much to do with insecurity as restraint. Guitarist Neil Hubbard and bassist John McKenzie are the epitome of discretion; indeed, for the first two lines of the song Rowland is accompanied only by Blair Cunningham's near-inaudible brushes.

The singer's delivery is bluffly humble, like a broken man painfully and slowly learning to walk again; he's trying to talk to her, to us, as best he can manage – the delivery is not refined, but it is a question of familiarizing oneself again with this sort of language so that the ability to love can be rediscovered ("my-heart-a-keeps-a-break-in'-ah"). Lush strings filter in from the left channel but are for now kept at a distance. Note the subtle changes to the lyrics – "you see, this guy" as opposed to "you say this guy," and "what I'd give to make you mine" rather than "what I'd do" – with a radical break at the first climax where, instead of offering death as an alternative option to himself, after "say you're in love, in love with this guy," he extends the "guyyyyyyyyyy" as though hanging onto an umbilical cord; then the music simply slides to a halt and he offers a simple, spoken "please."

The trumpet instrumental break is replaced by Mark Feltham's harmonica (we only hear a harmonica in the third and fourth lines of the first verse of Alpert's version) while Rowland repeats to himself "come on, come on" as he does throughout the album, willing himself to believe in his own restoration, begging himself to keep breathing. When he returns for the second and final chorus it is clear that he has gradually lost his reserve; his post-Russell Mael vibrato sites his voice at the edge of tears and total breakdown (the vulnerable tightrope is a major theme on the record), and for the last, and indeed, only time, he sings, very lowly, slowly and deliberately, that crucial line, stretching it out like a noose threatening to overlap the clothes line – "if not I'll just.........die," the "die" coming out as an exhausted bitonal baritone sob. Hubbard's guitar ripples his consent and concern, and the song "dies" into the bluer ether. Mercifully, he has not died.

4

Sally Shapiro: Hold Me So Tight

20 September 2007

This year's "Young Folks" but with added "Pacific State" input? Think spiraling oceans of synths, limpid modulations through heartbreaking chord changes, stout Cortez looking over the roof of the disco and finding Avalon. The noble, lucidly dreamt poignancy of Global Communications, Lawrence (the German techno one, not the Felt/Denim/Go-Kart Mozart chap), Casinos Versus Japan, Jeff Mills with his XL3 bathing cap on ... there is a certain kind of maximalistic, generously melodic techno to which I could listen and in which I could swim forever. Combine with the admirably hurt song structures of the Pet Shop Boys at their most distant (and yet, paradoxically, their closest) and a lyrical bent derived from the average C86 seven-inch, filtered via Saint Etienne when they let go and allow themselves to drift (side two of *Tiger Bay*, "How We Used To Live"), and you would have something like the six divinely felt minutes of "Hold Me So Tight."

Skeptics have questioned whether Sweden's Sally Shapiro actually exists, but there she is, photographed twice, beaming but cautious of eyes, on the cover of her *Disco Romance* CD; one Johan Agebjörn appears to be the principal musician, songwriter and producer behind her wary smile. It is New Pop, but not quite Annie or Abba, even though it is as happy to pause for extended thought as either. "I Will Be With You" may be the standout track (though for the time being I do not intend to discuss it publicly), but "Hold Me So Tight" is blessed with near equivalent magic.

Shivering its way into illuminated splendor out of an unspecified cold, Shapiro counterpoints the music's epic majesty with observations on how ordinary days and circumstances can lead to transcendence; she sings plaintively (and hesitatingly but affectingly in the upper range) about meeting her Other in a store ("you were in my way"); they get to talking "about the rain falling on the streets" and end up as "friends meeting twice a week." In the bridge the chord changes double in speed to mimic her belatedly excited increased pulse rate ("I may be wrong but I may be true/But I think you like me too") before diving off the springboard into an Esther Williams eternity of a chorus, countering night ("I see a lantern shining bright/I know you'll be mine in no time in the moonshine" – note the ingenious triple internal rhyme used to bring the chorus to the first of its two rhetorical climaxes) with day ("So be mine in the sunshine"). The music waxes and wanes as they dance in the club and internal fireworks explode – "I looked into your eyes, you gave me a smile.../And nothing else existed for a while," Shapiro sings as though she wants nothing else to exist, ever – before the song comes back into focus, not afraid to absent the beats for half a verse at a time, constantly altering its perspective, finally letting the glorious melody take over, dissolve and rekindle in volcanoes of benign borealis. So the small ("we were never meant to go walking along") is turned into the immortal; the death of New Pop is deferred yet again, and another great song attracts me to its attention at the time when I needed to find it.

5

Pink Floyd: Apples And Oranges

27 September 2007

The Floyd would probably prefer it if I didn't talk about "Apples And Oranges." In the first edition of the Guinness Book Of Top 40 Charts "Another Brick In The Wall Part II" is described as their first UK single release since "See Emily Play," and most of their fans accept this to be the case. But there was one further single, towards the end of 1967, as Syd was maneuvering himself towards the exit door. "Apples And Oranges" has become the great unmentionable item in the otherwise seamless Floyd discography; deemed by most involved parties at the time to be an irredeemable mess, neither the band nor EMI went out of their way to promote it, relatively few copies were pressed, it received virtually no radio play, did not trouble the Top 50 and was quickly deleted in a presumed attempt to save face. Although its B-side "Paintbox" resurfaced on Relics, the A-side didn't, and since then it has only been made available on a very few occasions, as part of a bonus CD included with an extravagantly priced retrospective boxed set, as one of six tracks on a blink-and-you-missed-it stand alone CD EP, and most recently as part of the bonus third disc of the deluxe 40th anniversary edition of *Piper At The Gates Of Dawn*, which has now (in London at any rate) sold out its limited run. Rather than an embarrassment to be swept speedily under the *Saucerful Of Secrets* carpet, it is perhaps a final tribute to Syd and to "Apples And Oranges" that the track now sounds utterly contemporary. To make a completely unoriginal comparison, it sounds like late nineties Blur; a vaudeville swagger undermined and detoured by wayward guitar and unexpected interludes. Today it doesn't sound at all unusual – Syd's eager chasing of the girl around town ("Feeling good at the top/Shopping in sharp shoes/Walking in the sunshine town feeling very cool") actually summing up the dying days of King's Road psychedelia with great acuity, while his guitar roars and snaps on the sidelines before the band land graciously on the harmonies of the song's title as chorus, followed by an extended pregnant quaver of uncertain guitar drones before abruptly veering back into the second verse as Syd tries to get closer to her – "I catch her by the eye then I stop and have to think/What a funny thing to do 'cos I'm feeling very pink."

This then gives way to a gorgeous, semi-tortured sequence of proto-blissout with Syd's "I love she, she loves me," the group's escalating triple "see you"s; bridged by the most ecstatic of collective swoons, Richard Wright's electric piano introduces a wedding bells motif which Syd's guitar picks up immediately, followed by Waters' sliding bass, some more ruminative guitar chimes, and finally a hallucinatory antiphonal choir and church organ turning the Chelsea girl into a hymn. For the final stretch, Syd utters an emphatic, ecstatic "Thought you might like to KNOW!" before informing us that "I'm her lorry driver man," still watching her, now perhaps a little more sinisterly ("She's on the run/down by the riverside/Feeding ducks in the afternoon tide" – immediately answered by a group "quack, quack") before the final chorus, which itself dissolves into a curious Cockney scat singing segment, some Goon-type nonsense syllables and a final high-pitched feedback signoff. On the *Piper* bonus disc, the tune appears in both mono and (for the first time) stereo mixes; at the end of the latter Syd assures the rest of the group, somewhat poignancy given his eventual fate, "I'll explain it all to you sometime … one day." He never did, but as with that other Hurricane Smith-produced masterpiece of late 1967 psych-pop, "Defecting Grey" by the Pretty Things, he seemed to approach "Apples And Oranges" with a brief strictly to have as much experimental fun as possible, and it deserves permanent rescue from the sub-carpet debris.

6

Funky Monkey: Peaceman

I October 2007

The musical factor which tends to make me most homesick for 1967 is that of the gargantuan, opulently compressed orchestra. There's been a lot of reminiscing on radio of late with the 40th anniversaries of Radios 1 and 2 and the concurrent demise of pirate radio, but it's the hugeness, the cavernous echoes, which speak to me most dearly – think of George Martin's original "Theme One" (described by a veteran BBC producer at the time, and not altogether disapprovingly, as "William Walton gone mad") or David Sinclair Whitaker's 16 rpm reworking of "The Last Time" (later the foundation of "Bitter Sweet Symphony") or Mark Wirtz's piccolo trumpets, harpsichords and Home Service strings on "Excerpt From A Teenage Opera". And that's without mentioning Wally Stott and Peter Knight's work on the first Scott Walker album, let alone "A Day In The Life." Of their time, yet simultaneously behind and ahead of it, this music still speaks to me of promises – some fulfilled, others trampled over in the progress of time.

"Peaceman" inspires similar feelings in me; if Radio Caroline had still been a going concern in 1998/9, I could well imagine their using this as a station ID, or an anthem. Funky Monkey – which seems essentially to have been producer and sometime Saint Etienne collaborator Gerard Johnson – were one of a thousand Big Beat hopefuls of the period; their records were diverting (extra chutzpah points for including the original, undiluted Oliver Nelson *Six Million Dollar Man* theme on their debut, *Come Together People Of Funk*) if not especially radical, and apart from the unsatisfactory compilation *Join Us In Tomorrow,* with a considerably inferior six-minute mix of "Peaceman," their work has vanished from the racks.

No, "Peaceman" must be heard in its original, slowly unfolding, ten-minute, ten-second version. It begins with a Bach prelude played on a string synth which is steadily engulfed by the sound of riots and police sirens; a police radio voiceover ("Big shanks, good shanks"?) is turned into the foundation of the track as the beats systematically make their entrance; first one rhythm, then a grittier overlay, followed by electric piano and bass. Comparisons with Primal Scream's "Come Together" would not be farfetched, except "Peaceman" is faster and slightly brighter.

An intriguing harmonic sequence is developed by the electric piano (using the initially cited Bach melodic sequence as a springboard) and the bass over the now danceable rhythm, until, at 4:45, the sunrise of synthesized strings, playing a gorgeously painful major/minor melody, casts its yellow shadow over the proceedings. A rhythm breakdown follows until the melody re-enters, reinforced, at 6:47, followed at 7:22 by Denise Johnson's voice (hence the Primal Scream connection) singing, or intoning, "Come together, people of funk." I think of Number 6, freed and back in London, on the verge of tears as he surveys the Houses of Parliament and the South Bank, with "Peaceman"'s swelling melody in my ears and mind. Listening to it is like standing on top of Parliament Hill Fields as the clouds steadily begin to clear, the Highgate church spire behind me, the city ahead of me ...it is lump in the throat time. Finally the music fades away to leave the electric pianist (billed on the credits as "Vegas Love") improvising on the chord sequence (cf. Anne Dudley's piano at the end of the album version of Art of Noise's "Beat Box") before drifting into another song altogether and then swiftly ending with a final flourish. A masterpiece which deserves salvation from wherever you can find it.

7

Paolo Conte: La Casa Cinese

2 October 2007

Paolo Conte reminds me of my dad. He looks nothing like him, and likes his cigarettes whereas my dad was a stalwart pipe man, but there is that same golden, verging on auburn, Sunday autumn morning melancholy about his bearing. But 2004's *Elegia* album feels like the expression of an encroaching melancholy from which there is no return; although he turns seventy this year, it still seems premature to view *Elegia* as his last word, since his partial Montreal doppelganger Leonard Cohen remains firmly productive fifteen years after recording "Waiting For The Miracle". But there is a sense of deep hurt and loss throughout the recital, words about wanting to be hugged and held if he can't get his music back, wondering what he would do if he lost it. In a lot of ways he is what Serge Gainsbourg might have turned into had he survived to seventy and developed a mournful perspective on his life and the world, physical and aesthetic, which ensured his birth. I am sure that Conte, as with Gainsbourg (and Van Morrison), had his youthful ear firmly cupped to the steam radio, waiting for AFN's *Stars Of Jazz* to filter through the static; Bird and Diz, Miles and Sonny, an escape from his banal surroundings, even though he remains a citizen of his original birthplace of Asti.

Some of *Elegia* is typically very funny, including the marvelous "Frisco" where he lopes along, semi-drunk, valuing the Bay as an ancient wonder more precious than Memphis or Luxor while his band warm up on some old Don Redman charts behind him. But most of it seems to find him retaining only the scarcest hold on life, his world and sanity. "La Casa Cinese" – "The Chinese House" – is a comparatively miniaturist piece but in its stark abnegation of wonder is as bleak as anything on the current PJ Harvey album. Over doggedly anchored piano and double bass he looks at the man – or is it a mirror image of himself? – "searching for a street...here's a naked soul. . ." while the chorus is an agonised, gravelly hum soundtracked by a poignant, Carla Bley-ish clarinet top line. "Just what are you searching for over there? There's the Chinese house ... painted blue ..."; the lyrics are helpfully printed in French and English in the CD booklet as well as the original Italian, so I must point out the subtle reference to "Volare" which his performance gives in that "painted blue". At the "blue" a sudden avalanche of agitated strings makes itself known before dying back down, receding into the darkening gloom ("This darkness doesn't help/If anything, it forgives us..."). He wonders how much the changes in his life have negated, or strengthened, his original desire ("Memory is enchanted/Yes, that's what you want.../Thoughts that no longer apply/Have you changed them? I don't know"), but finally knows that the Grail he seeks has long since vanished, or possibly never even existed: "You're asking me about a street/Anything you like/But the Chinese house/That you won't find." Or, translated into a chant I used to hear in my Glasgow youth all the time: "If you'd've been where I'd've been you would've seen the Fairy Queen!" And then Gauguin's *Nevermore*. The piano steadily winds the song down like a music box coming to the end of its programmed pirouette; has he the energy to wind it up again? At my dad's age, I think I understand the feeling now.

8

East River Pipe: Party Drive

9 October 2007

FM Cornog has put out many albums under the East River Pipe name, and will doubtless continue to do so; but 1999's *The Gasoline Age* is the one which has stuck with me. It is the record I have turned to for those especially lonesome, auburn-lit journeys; at the time, Thursday mornings on the 400 bus to Headington, walking the last ten minutes to the John Radcliffe Hospital for my weekly physiotherapy, cars slow, no one really about, or lunchtime Oxford Tube coaches back home, not in a rush, but the mind in a mess; ominous sunny mornings in Abingdon, Saturday lunchtime bus rides to unfathomable places like Tolworth. Or the number 11 bus, cruising through the nearly empty City before coming to rest at the temporarily abandoned Liverpool Street terminal. Times when you've no real places to go and you're looking to grasp something but as yet haven't quite worked out what.

The Gasoline Age is like that; 45 minutes of sedate, secluded cruising through electroindie dreams of motion, coming to a wasted but gracious halt in some unspecified bypass within walking distance of time. The nearly ten-minute delicate climax of "Atlantic City (Gonna Make A Million Tonight)" is the record's probable masterpiece, an ineffable arch of sadness; but "Party Drive" has remained my personal favorite (though really the album needs to be experienced as a whole, continuous entity). With lugubrious synthesizers and drum machines which recall nothing so much as the Springsteen of *Tunnel Of Love* – simultaneously his sleekest and most desolate record – Cornog sings, in an unsteady bass croon rising to a slightly more confident contralto, about driving away, driving anywhere, as the music proceeds in a stately manner behind him with intensely moving chord changes while the lyric systematically debunks Motley Crue-type concepts of "partying"; he sings words like "Cigarettes, cans of beer/Piled up in the rear," "Route 26? Or 22?/A joint for me, pills for you" and "Summer nights, no cops in sight" but he sings of a wounded retreat rather than triumphalist Porkyisms. They're off somewhere, or perhaps to nowhere, the destination less feared than the starting point – "You can break my bones, but don't take me home!" he pleads repeatedly, "Just drive – the party drive." He sounds as though he is being driven to the edge of the world, afraid of what he might see if he dares to peer over. A beautiful study of solitude which reminds me why I never want to be alone again.

9

Lesley Duncan: Love Song

11 October 2007

The early seventies weren't just about the glam. They were about the successive hangovers from the sixties (artistically) and the thirties (socially – walk in and around the Glasgow of 1973 and it might as well have been 1933; everyone firmly in some other time's place), about the whispered dread of imminent apocalypse, huddled up in a blanketed corner, about kids from the Catholic school trying to run you over with their bikes, about the loss of power, about black and white, oranges squashed with a hammer and other public safety horror films, about trying not to die ...

... about picking up the pieces, about finding the resources and the will to make new ones, about things and people left over from '67, about Lesley Duncan, whose songs I heard on Radio 2 all the time as a child when not drowned out by the brand new roar of the Zanussi washing machine, who may have appeared on *The Two Ronnies* or similar *Shows Of The Week*, about grasping something before it becomes lost forever ...

"The words I have to say may well be simple but they're true..."

... about her "Love Song," which has subsequently been covered by everyone in the world, from Elton John to Olivia Newton-John, from Julio Iglesias to Pitman, but none of these, but none, touches the stranded strand of the original, as sung and performed by the writer herself ...

... about her record trying not to be a record, about it sounding as remote a ghost in 2007 as Blind Willie Johnson's "Dark Was The Night" even though she is still here, but it sounds like a refugee from an elapsed time capsule, as if she just picked up the guitar in the corner of her kitchen and sang the song while the world spun around her, about the ironically jaunty whistling at the beginning of the record, welcoming a new day not everyone wished to see, and Lesley Duncan, her voice resonant and firm but not harsh, gently asking for the whole scenario to be pummeled to bits ("Until you give your love, there's nothing more that we can do"), asking her '67 people not to forget '67 ("Love is what we came here for/No one could offer you more...do you know what I mean? Have your eyes really seen?"), knowing that nettles have to be grasped and that fear of scratches outweighs living death ("You say it's very hard to leave behind the life we knew/But there's no other way, and now it's really up to you"). Electric piano flurries kiss the stale air like doves wearing down a blockade of smog ...

*"Love is the key we must turn. Truth is the flame we must burn. Freedom the lesson we must learn. **Do you know what I mean?**"*

... about the singer vanishing into her own song, the cars and buses passing by outside her third floor window, the barely audible exchanges downstairs, past the close and out into the street ("Please miss," "Next time round"), about the jangling of keys or is it spare change, about taking the money, about preferring to take the chance and run, about not gluing ourselves to a world now spent ..." Well, play something on the piano" as an old lady, probably older than the century, croaks out the sincerest "Lili Marlene" she's ever heard and it's time to go, about the cupboard exploding, about time running out, about not always leaving all options open, about Jessica Niblick, about what if Lesley Duncan's name had been Vashti Bunyan, about all of us moving or wanting to move in the same direction, about striding out from beneath the blankets of blue, about dusting down the portholes, about opening them up and breathing in roses ... a shilling in the meter and a deposit for the palace of the future ... do you know what I mean? Have your eyes really been seen?

Blur: Popscene

12 October 2007

The beginning of Britpop time, marooned in an era which did not yet have the time for it, "Popscene" was barely acknowledged – another shoegazer hourglass licking the final atoms of sand was the general shoulder-shrug reaction – and as with that other 1992 single which promised a future for pop but which few at the time heeded, "Avenue" by Saint Etienne, glanced half-heartedly into the Top 40 (one week at number 32 over Easter) before driving off in a huff. Although Blur have continued to perform the song live, they treated "Popscene" as the record Britain didn't deserve; it is conspicuously absent from *Modern Life Is Rubbish* – though does appear on the American and Japanese editions – and from the *Best Of Blur* compilation.

Revving up like a lawnmower fighting the wasp back, or a motor not yet headed anywhere, Graham Coxon's self-swamping guitars provoke a determinedly stern Mod-punk rhythm before the mighty central riff is declaimed by masses of brass, glide guitar and near unnoticeable harmonium (the latter two stay for the verses). Then Damon appears to spit at whatever dream has been lost ("A fervored image of another world is nothing in particular now"), accusing British rock of settling for limp MBV/Nirvana xeroxes ("And everyone is a clever clone/A chrome colored clone am I"), hammering against the Camden Underworld toilet door of indifference ("Just repeat this again and again ... and aGAAAAIN!") before sneering his ball of demolition in the chorus ("Hey, hey, come out tonight...PopSCENE! All RIGHT!!").

Coxon's guitar "solo" does its best to erase the song while Damon speaks of running away from cliché only to find another cliché ("No queues and no panic there/Just dangling your feet in the grass"); he doesn't quite know what he's aiming for yet ("My lack of natural lustre now/Seems to be losing me friends") but wants, needs it to be better than the scene which celebrates French fisherman's stripy jumpers ("So in the absence of a way of life...").

"Popscene" is a monstrous call to arms, and the irony of its aptness in relation to the 1996/7 post-Britpop ruination need not be underlined. Yet its commercial and critical failure may be more ascribable to the fact that, judging by what else was in that April Top 40 which wasn't the product of dinosaurs or bland American Idol antecedents, there was a pop scene in full flourish, namely rave and everything which stemmed and arose from it. It's possible that Albarn was calling for "rock" to take this on, in spirit if not in form, but few were in the mood to heed Albarn's calls; in that year's Rollercoaster tour, which also involved Dinosaur Jr, MBV and the Mary Chain, Blur seemed to be uninterestedly making up the numbers. But still, that motor had started up, and the journey across the Westway and back into the heart of something couldn't be delayed for much longer.

Mari Wilson & the Wilsations: Baby It's True

16 October 2007

Almost a decade and a half ahead of Mike Flowers, there were Neasden, and beehives, and Mari Wilson; a #42 hit in the shining month of New Pop that was May 1982, "Baby It's True" was probably prohibited from climbing any further by having its tongue stuck slightly too firmly in its cheek – the deadpan Home Counties spoken intro, including the immortal tag line: "It's been a long time since I saw my baby – in fact … I can hardly remember what he looks like" – but is still Mari's masterpiece, and also that of writer Teddy Johns, as a (relatively) mainstream follow-up to the still extraordinarily adventurous "Beat The Beat," a #59 hit from earlier in the year composed by Tot Taylor and initiating a Sondheim New Pop perspective which nobody appears to have followed up.

As a simulacrum of 1968 CBS Brit bubblegum aspiring to Motown, "Baby It's True" is hard to beat; from its opening cyclical bassline, soon joined and doubled up by lead guitar – a line so good it crops up largely unaltered in the Belle Stars' top three hit "Sign Of The Times" eight months later – the layers of keyboards, drums, alto sax and strings are steadily applied, and once Wilson gets past her "out there in Radioland" spiel, the song opens up with its Sisyphean staircase of unrequited absence ("I CAN'T/Stop MY/Self FROM/LO-VING-you and/I CAN'T…"); she sings the first verse's quintuplet of "baby, baby, baby, baby, baby" as though falling down that staircase backwards in slow motion, or even reluctantly tap dancing her way back down the stairs. After the second chorus, she absents herself briefly to make way for an extremely May 1982 arrangement of salsa(ish) beats, Gary Kemp guitar and Harry Beckett trumpet (which sounds as though Beckett may have played the solo himself; compare and contrast with Weekend's "View From Her Room" from the same month) before gliding back in with a deftly agonized "I NEED you too!" and renewing her pleas for the absent Other to answer her prayer and make her so very happy (all those references and subtexts gradually accumulating) before the final, glorious, key-changing ascent of the chorus into the shiny yellow stratosphere with Wilson's joyful high-note exclamations of "I can't stop myself!" and then one more unexpected chord change, a flurry of Motown piccolos before the end with the bass droning and then sliding upwards and out like Marianne's motorcycle. "Baby It's True" transcends its own inbuilt irony, much as its smarter, richer Northern cousin "The Look Of Love" does; a Eurovision winner if anybody wants it, and a future number one single for any performer astute enough to seek it out.

The Blue Nile: Family Life

18 October 2007

Shadows of differing degrees of silver – the moon, the icicles – filter through most of Alan Spence's *Its Colours They Are Fine*. A novel, a meditation disguised as a collection of short stories about growing up, growing old and growing out in and of Glasgow, it was published in 1977 and I recognized its chimes of limitation. Starting with a childhood Christmas, impoverished and to a degree frustrated but still obtaining magic by means of innate goodness, and moving onward to the multiple disappointments and revelations which the rest of life will furnish; Shuggie, already doomed at eighteen, lashing out jealously at love rivals in the 1968 dancehall but still spellbound and transmuted by the power of the music he hears – Motown, "This Old Heart Of Mine" – the confusions and misplaced pride in Glasgow's ongoing religious apartheid system (the book's title comes from an old Orange Lodge marching song), the internal and external rebellions of a cross-religious wedding, the drift towards other, less easily definable worlds until the book ends about one street away from where it began but in a separate universe; the spirit finding its own nexus and axis.

And, above all, the story "The Palace," about the middle-aged man, recently widowed, living in furnished rooms, waiting for life to reshow itself, finding small but immense magic in the second-hand markets, or just sitting in the Kibble Palace at the Botanic Gardens ... waiting and perhaps praying quite a lot more than he is prepared to let on ...

Much of this permeates "Family Life". On every Blue Nile

album there is a moment where time is literally stopped and emotions laid open and bare. On *A Walk Across The Rooftops* it was "Easter Parade"; on *Hats* it was "From A Late Night Train" (with its unconscious reminders of Hardy's "On A Heath"). *Peace At Last*, the third Blue Nile album, came out in 1996 and received a muted reaction – the consensus was that they had become too glossy – but "Family Life," buried deep at its core, is the cynosure of all of the group's work, and I would argue that unless you grew up in Glasgow at a certain time you will be able to understand and inhabit the song only up to a point.

It's Christmas Eve, and Paul Buchanan's narrator is too ashamed even to let God look at him ("Starlight do you know me? Please don't look at me now ... I'm falling apart ...") but still he prays, his murmur frequently faltering into tears. "Jesus, love ...let me down ... and I know where you are ... it might lead somewhere . . ." The song has to form around his emotion; it sounds as though he is watering a spring flower, out of season but perfect, in a cracked vase on a rotting sill. "Jesus, please ...(he can scarcely resume going on at this point) make us happy sometimes ... no more shout ... no more fight ... family life."

Note the singularity of that "shout" as though it is a person, a bogeyman, a demon which shatters all hope of goodness under that trembling roof. I do not recount how many times such thoughts flooded through my childhood mind.

But this isn't quite the portrait of a boy wanting his mum and dad to get on and actually love each other, even if the narrator may be recalling his own childhood. "Tomorrow will be Christmas," Buchanan sings with the heaviest sigh of dread any singer has ever applied to the season ... the façade of the old songs, the pseudo-merry, and still the simmering hatred ...

At the third "Jesus" – "Jesus, you ..." – his voice swallows itself and he literally cannot go on; the piano continues to pick out the patient melody, with discreet strings weeping in the background ... but somehow he manages to finish this entreaty:

"Wipe the tears from her face/And the sound of his voice" ...
think about that latter; is he asking Jesus to wipe the sound of
his voice. Does he – or she? - fear hearing it so much?

It is possible that each verse may be prayed from the
perspective of a different narrator – husband, then child, then
wife – or that it is all coming from the mind of this one
tormented (and tormenting?) man who may himself be the
cause of all the pain. At the end the whole song crouches down
to allow his slow but vital breath: "Jesus, I go to sleep and I pray
... for my kids ... for my wife ... family life." I'm sure such
thoughts flooded through his adult mind, too. Would that have
excused what happened? Are we being asked to empathize or at
least sympathize with a man who is substantially less than
straightforward – or does he honestly feel that it's all happening
to him and this is why he...? But then – the whitening joy of
Christmas lights, the soft candor of her touch in what was not a
proper bed as such but it would do and they find peace within
each other and let the bombs fall elsewhere, the elapsed
evolution, the journey upwards and out of the mundane
towards the nearly definable other – so leave a prayer for my
dad too while you're at it, because he didn't get many in his life.
I am only seven years behind him now but in all other senses a
million miles away.

13

Simon Warner: Waiting Rooms

19 October 2007

Active in music for nearly a quarter of a century but only venturing into the public gaze with acute rarity, 1997's *Waiting Rooms* is as yet the only Simon Warner album; a pained, and at times very funny, account of overaged bedsit life set to Richard Benbow's prosperous orchestrations which had the misfortune of coming out just as the Divine Comedy were at their critical and commercial peak; there wasn't room for two lush avant-balladeers, although there seemed to be room aplenty for scores of mirthless post-Oasis Britrockers.

But the album seems to be both prelude and epilogue to "Waiting Rooms," the song; it opens with Warner busking it, at one end or the other of the Victoria-Brighton line, humming into his wary acoustic guitar, and ends with a distant string chorale and an even more distant howl as he returns home, brews up a cup, lights up and switches the answerphone on for the evening. One Daphne Warner, who I presume is his mother, contributes mezzo-soprano backing, while Benbow's strings climb ominously and descend reluctantly behind Warner's recounting of the "scuffed snaps" of his mother he has just found; cinders of Chanel girl flashbacks, admission of a full and purposeful life having been lived . . .but now, a curious emptiness as she, or he, wanders alone through these increasingly dusty and empty passageways, life having spent most of its own bounty – "She's not at home! This home is haunted!" Warner growls with ineffable sadness (but not pity) as the orchestra repeatedly opens up and folds upon his smoky musings. "Waiting for . . .nothing but . . .time," he hisses like a prematurely aged David Essex, ushering in a music box: "Vulgar and dusted, an antique zone," which in turn leads to the strings and horns sweeping in again like not yet purulent vultures. But wherever he, or she, wanders, the loss, the absence, is inescapable; "but each new home feels like a train station waiting room." The swallowing feeling that he, and perhaps we, should be elsewhere instead of trespassing on our own willfully suppressed ghosts. We need to know what happened in the intervening decade. Did he get out, and annul that faint Newley aroma of declining dissonance?

14

The Serpent Power: Endless Tunnel

25 October 2007

All I knew about the eponymous debut album by the Serpent Power – note the suggestion of *Sgt Pepper* in that name – before finding a copy and listening to it was that Christgau rated it the 28th best album of 1967 and I wanted to know why; they made further records, but this is the only one remotely findable in the UK, and indeed finding it was a remote and lengthy pursuit. Leader David Meltzer (whose wife Tina appears on co-lead vocals – I have no idea whether either is related to Richard but am presuming not since they do not appear anywhere in *The Aesthetics Of Rock*) is a noted second-stage Beat Generation poet, and some of that is evident in the poems printed on the album's sleeve (one haikuesque offering, "27 April 67," reads:

> *"No one to write to*
> *but to myself tonight*
> *Not even the familiar phantom*
> *behind my chair*
> *Who scans all words for immortality"*).

Musically, however, The Serpent Power offer what on the surface is something fully to be expected from early '67 SF; a mixture of post-Yardbirds frat blues yowling (with David doing the yowling – check out his splendidly boyish tantrum on "Nobody Blues": "I'm gonna walk into my closet ... and I'm gonna shut the door ... and I'm gonna cry! .. .I'm gonna SOB!" which is all the more effective by coming directly after Tina's wistful "Flying

Away" in which she threatens "If you tell me one more lie/I will run away and cry") with John Payne digging into his Mysterians organ, hopeful Monkees/Mamas and Papas-type anthems to the new spiritual sunrise (mostly sung by both David and Tina – from "Open House": "The black cloud's moved away! . . .Open up your door!") and ethereal folky musings (mostly sung by Tina, who only really loses her immaculate, pre-Linda Perhacs cool towards the end of "Forget," when she sighs "Oh I HATE tomorrow!"). Unlike, say, the Velvets, the music doesn't scream RADICAL in the listener's face, and the first few listens may lead to naught beyond a shrug of the shoulders, but there are other subtly restless factors at work; the unexpected harmonic amplifications of "Gently, Gently," where the group doggedly descend down the semitone scale, the harmonic ambiguity which greets the "Forever!"s of "Open House" and at times even points a generation ahead to Tortoise. Its less than formal (or legal?) atmosphere leads to tracks being faded almost randomly, as though merely recording excerpts from a performance too long to fit into 40 over-convenient minutes.

But "Endless Tunnel" was the big finish to the record, the standard epic raga/mindblowing freakout. Except in its thirteen or so minutes it never really freaks out. Here David offers the usual metaphor of train journey as passage to who knows where, and gets increasingly frantic in his requests: "Oh Mister Conductor, tell we where are we going? . . .But Mister Conductor, he just walked on by," until he resorts to petulant, extended squeals of frustration over the lack of an answer as he proceeds through the train, car by car, passing through cobras and pythons who "hissed out a welcome," hawks pecking out his eyes, platoons of ladies looking for a lover, and so forth. The sort of thing which in normal circumstances would fully deserve standing in the corner and writing a hundred lines.

It came out a few months ahead of "The End" and the similarities are marked (though there is no climax as such) but in truth it's much more fun and enterprising than dull old Jimbo and his Oedipal integrity kick; everyone digs in for the instrumental sections, none more so than one J P Pickens, who guests on "electrified 5-string banjo" and wails up a storm with his plucking, nearly walking away with the track (you'll believe that a banjo can scream) before Meltzer's lead guitar comes in to plot a more considered route to its orgasm, with his characteristic rapid, blunt picking of notes as though he is attempting to use his guitar to wax and pluck Ralph Gleason's moustache. He audibly realizes the absurdity of the journey halfway through – you can hear him turning over his lyric sheet – but continues to go for it anyway; with "bloodlike lake water seeping through my shoes" he tries to gain access to the engineer's cabin, offering every conceivable variation on the "let me in" motif, and when he is finally let in and asks the engineer, again, where we are going, he turns round, grins and replies "I don't know … I'm just following the tracks … up and down the tracks …" whereupon both train and song speed out of the picture. Try and track the whole album down, though; already its tracks are bearing that sense of near-instant familiarity that makes you want to listen to it in its entirety. OK, maybe it's 1967's 37th best album. For now.

15

J Walter Negro & the Loose Jointz: Shoot The Pump

29 October 2007

It should have been one of the great summer dance hits, possibly even a necessary balance to the following summer's "The Message." "Shoot The Pump" is a joyous ode to fire hydrant violation and subsequent ejaculation of spray as barely concealed sexual metaphor ("Wow, you got that chick wet all the way across the street, Seeley!" J Walter Negro congratulates lead guitarist Leonard K Seeley Jnr, following the mother of all ejaculatory guitar solos, half-Hendrix, half-Sharrock), not quite hip hop, not quite downtown No Wave, not quite post-Ze Latin postmodernism, which should have squirted all over the charts – but Island Records gingerly flung it onto the British market in mid-December 1981 and it was inevitably drowned beneath the considerably more powerful sprays of the Christmas rush, having yet to materialize on CD over a quarter of a century later.

If Carla Bley had been musical director of Kid Creole and the Coconuts they might have sounded like "Shoot The Pump"; indeed sometime Bley organist Arturo O'Farrill contributes a suitably unhinged, reverb-drenched Hammond solo to the track. And its seemingly good-natured spring is devoted to a celebration of flooding the neighborhood and the finer arts of graffiti and culminates in an over-hasty police shooting ("Oh my God! It was only a monkey wrench!").

These days such a scenario would be illustrated with sub-John Carpenter synth ominosities, doomy, throaty raps and perhaps an obscure-ish Blue Magic sample. But "Shoot The

Pump"'s good humor proves to be indestructible, since the shooting victim has been wearing a bulletproof vest ("Oh, I'm gonna live forever or die tryin'," he remarks casually, scarcely three minutes after the track has been nearly obscured by police sirens, outraged yells of "get away from that fire hydrant ya punk, don't ya know there's a WATER shortage!" and gunfire, as J Walter returns to the sprightly avant-bubblegum with which he started, full of the inevitable double entendres ("Then you turn up the pressure and then you turn up the funk/You put the spray in the can and then you shoot the pump," followed in the second verse by a sly [or Sly] "Uh, you do know how to twist and shout, don't you baby?" and, near the end, a purr of "That's why they call me the plain brown rapper").

The horns (one of whom, Eric Leeds, went on to become Prince's regular saxman, and there's certainly more than an element of purple portent here) are sunny, the handclaps childlike and yellow, the rhythm easy but insistent – Tomas Doncker's supporting guitar instantly reversing me to 1981, vibrant bass from Lonnie Hillyer Jr, son of the Mingus trumpeter, to remind us that everything connects and continues – the adventure inherent and enormous. Sadly, from what I've been able to find out online, J Walter Negro's story proved a partially fallacious one and ultimately a sad one – he appears to have died from drug abuse some years ago – and yet "Shoot The Pump" is a tightrope of a reminder when things weren't quite set in stone and musicians from different fields could work with each other and create something truly new. Keep it next to your *Mutant Disco*, *Was (Not Was)*, *Memory Serves*, "Genius Of Love" and *Electric Spanking Of War Babies* and marvel at how such music could make even winter sound sunny.

16

Dorothy Squires: My Way

30 October 2007

The most popular song to be played at funerals, or at least it was in those pre-Whitney/Robbie/Celine days, "My Way" has functioned as a kneejerk safety valve, celebrating the independence and fulfillment of those who spent their whole lives kneeling, embedded in numbing and often humiliating day jobs where the average cockroach crawling midway up the staff room walls had more say about its fate and they ever did. It is the expression of a wish never granted.

Most singers who think of themselves as big (or small) have essayed the song in its lifetime (though Whitney, Robbie and Celine have yet to avail us of their readings), usually with one of two results: somewhat smug and self-satisfied, or loudly defiant. Sinatra himself remained ambivalent about the song and his own delivery of it, and indeed he adds that final coda where everything trickles into quietude, rather than culminating in a triumphantly loud flourish – "Yes … it was …my way," and the grain of his throat holds those last two words with as much suppressed despair as he ever mustered (the shattering "can know my sadness" which ends "None But The Lonely Heart" and the *No One Cares* album symbolizes the seeping of reluctant blood from the mourning wrist, when despair can no longer be contained). The single was not an especially big hit in the States – it peaked at #27, didn't hang around for long and in his book, *Dino,* Nick Tosches remarks how the Rat Pack boys were effectively ostracized from the pop charts by the late sixties and relegated to the cozy ghetto of the specialist Easy

Listening lists. But in Britain it gained a slowly gathering newness of life – it climbed agilely to number five on our charts soon after its April 1969 debut and then refused to exit, not taking its final bow until the beginning of 1972. Its cumulative run of 122 weeks remains the only triple digit run in the singles chart, far ahead of callow pretenders like "Amazing Grace," "Blue Monday" and "Chasing Cars," and if a full Top 75 had been in operation at the time the 200 mark would not have been inconceivable.

There was, of course, an underlying sense of reproach about "My Way"'s continued presence, as the sixties congealed into the seventies and the Engelbert/Valium/cooking sherry generation began to feel vindicated. See, they seemed to say, you only knew the half of our pain; this song, this man, says our lives are justified, however we live them. Do you think you're the only one who couldn't find their way home? And, as the seventies solidified into the eighties, we reached the other end of the spectrum; Elvis, already too careless to live, sung it from just beyond our grasp, and Sid, who as Paul Anka astutely noted seemed to turn the song from a passive reflection on passing away into an active weapon to speed up his passing. But nobody ever sang "My Way" without meaning it, even if the contradictions of their own semi-wrecked, semi-surrendered lives told them vividly to the contrary. Least of all Dorothy Squires, who recorded what I still believe to be the most truthful and disturbing interpretation of the song. Her "My Way" appeared as a single in the summer of 1970, shortly after she had invested five thousand pounds of her own money to stage a lavish comeback performance at the London Palladium. She was then fifty-five years old, and her life had been teetering towards wreckage for some time; a considerable star in the pre-rock era – her former partner, songwriter Billy Reid, composed "I'm Walking Behind You" especially for her (Eddie Fisher's chart-topping 1953 reading was a cover) – she married Roger Moore, a decade her junior, who left her in the early sixties for an Italian woman. She never really recovered from the latter; and it wasn't until the end of the sixties, after many bitter battles, that she granted Moore a divorce. By then drink had taken hold and her career was in serious decline.

However, as befitting someone born in a trailer park in Wales during WWI and who grew up during the Depression, she did not yield easily; fearful of ending up where she'd started on one hand, but casually reckless with resources and emotions on the other, she booked the Palladium, coming on with immense, garish, pastel-colored feather bows, unbowed and unapologetic. Like Judy, the voice wasn't quite what it had been, but the determination was violently visible, her audiences ready to suffer along with her and cheer her on as required.

Thus her "My Way"; a more garish, luminous, enraged version is scarcely imaginable still. She starts low, like Shirley Bassey, rolling her rich Welsh diphthongs and refusing to drop them. But she is like a huge mansion trembling atop a volcano, as when the lava orchestra swells up for her "And there were times – and I am sure that you knew," her voice already tearful in that second half, enunciating every individual syllable so that the listener cannot avoid receiving her message, still grieving for her lost love, but doggedly she will stand on top of that mountain regardless of any imminent eruption – "I ATE IT UP," she proclaims, and then, after a meaningful pause, she howls demonically, "AND! I! SPIT! IT! OUT!," with epileptic pitch control but putting all of the emotional emphasis on that "I." The Palladium audience was already in tears at her defiance of imminent and immense ruination.

Then she descends again – "I've laughed" she weeps – before attempting her second ascent, not even bothering to change the gender of the "For what is a man?" section (singing directly at her Roger? "WHAT HAS HE GOT?"), and now she is in charge, reigns supreme: "I TOOK THE BLOWS – AND! I! DID! IT! MY!

WAY!" That final "WAY!" sees her toppling from her precarious perch of pitching as though tumbling down the cliff to her irrevocable doom, but she greets her presumed demise with neither fear nor surprise, gracefully toppling like a newly swallowed gull. To add to her woes, the veteran tenor saxophonist Johnnie Gray provides an obbligato throughout her performance which sometimes seems to be laughing at her predicament (indeed he gets a co-credit on the label of the single) though his fleet descending bop runs at the climactic end seem also to indicate a sheer fall.

The record did well; although it only peaked at #25, it was on the chart for twenty-three weeks (eventually becoming one of the very few singles to earn a silver disc for 250,000 sales without ever breaking the Top 20), and its momentum helped in part to keep interest in Sinatra's original buoyant. But the demise turned out to be less than presumed. Squires' house burned down; underinsured, she vowed to move somewhere closer to the river, whereupon her next house was wrecked in a flood. Litigious at the touch of a button, most of her money went on fruitless High Court libel cases, all of which she lost; towards the end of her days (remarkably she soldiered on until 1998, aged eighty-three) she was rescued from destitution by a fan who put her up (and commendably, or foolishly, put up with her rages and whims) in her cottage in Yorkshire. But there is a rawness, a ghastly truth about her "My Way" which no other singer has yet approached, as though she stared right into its hollow heart and knew the lies it was telling, but embraced them anyway, because what was the alternative?

17

Ultrasound: Kurt Russell

I November 2007

Probably if Ultrasound hadn't been so relentlessly awkward they might have been contenders – alternatively, perhaps we should lament for times too strict and fearful to allow true awkwardness. They could have pruned down *Everything Picture*, their double album, to a jolly album of singalong indie (*Selected Picture?*), but that would have denied the enormity of mess vital to understanding their art. *Everything Picture* is sprawling and frequently mis-aimed, but the valiance of its very existence deserves praise. Not quite post-prog, not really post-shoegazing, nowhere as near to Britpop as Nude Records might perhaps have liked – a sleazier Suede? – and yet their bravery, or foolhardiness, should still command an element of admiration.

Their second single, "Best Wishes," its cover featuring a high street about to be submerged by floods, was their high mark, an extraordinary hymn to the departed and departing with solemn organ, hysterical guitar solos, earnest choirs, all of which ends in a whisper leading to a sustained guitar tone leading to two breaths leading to abrupt cutoff. It is not a song to which I return with frequency since its time – the spring of 1998 – was for me one of portents of impending demise which a few months later proved to be not entirely inaccurate.

I have kept the single as a reminder and a warning, but also because of its second track, "Kurt Russell," a number one had Suede been responsible for it – but singer/lyricist Andrew "Tiny" Woods was not one for Brett Anderson-style instant photogenicity; his pose was one of the most defiant in all of rock. And Woods had one of the great nineties rock voices, simultaneously vulnerable and bold: hear his forlornly swooning sigh on the "know" of the second verse's "'Cos you don't know you've been sold." He sings about shallow people ("They don't know that they're born") who are only interested in looks and presentation; never mind that "you're all evil," indeed "tell everybody you know" that you're evil, and somehow they'll admire you because, when it comes down to it, "We'll place our hands inside your pants" – Ultrasound's canon includes some of the best vocal harmony work of recent times (all from within the band themselves) and the semi-ironic counterpart to Woods' wistfully raging lead works brilliantly here with appropriate shivering chord changes.

"You're never gonna see me crawl/I'll always be there when you call/I want to be your hero/Kurt Russell, Eastwood and me," Woods declares in the chorus, over co-writer/guitarist Richard Green's post-McGuinn Rickenbacker peals which in the latter's solo fearlessly treads into Frampton-guitar-to-mouth territory. "You're never gonna see me cry," lies Woods, "I want to be your hero/Pacino, de Niro and me," which he himself answers with a bitterly ironic triplicate of "yeah"s, knowing that everything that makes A Man is virtual, non-existent. It ends again with a church organ sustenato which, again, abruptly rolls off the steeple, evading the dully complicated reality of being a human being.

18

Britney Spears: Heaven On Earth

5 November 2007

Whatever else *Blackout* may be, it's not Britney's *Low*. For one, that would have required a largely instrumental second half with cut-up and processed/distorted voices, and we only get the latter; the miniature Barthesian essay on the nature and expression of the word "baby" three-quarters of the way through "Perfect Lover" which uses only the word "baby," and the more pressing matter of Britney's ProTooled/Auto-detuned/stretched/squashed vocal grains throughout; the startling Godardian Cinemascope of the low, growled "More!"s in "Gimme More," Britney as her own man/lover in the parlous elegy of "Naked (I Got A Plan)," the logical next point of departure from Dee D Jackson's "Automatic Lover," the booming, low "LOW!" which intrudes into the "turn the lights down" quasi-fantasia of "Break The Ice."

For two, Britney does not sound especially low on this record (and for an incidental three, the lowing on this record sounds to me unambiguously Britney despite, or even because of, the multiple Berioesque variations which producers Bloodshy & Avant, Danja and co. apply to her voice(s)). Yes, there is the swipe at the press in "Piece Of Me" with its chain gang chorus of multiple facets of Britney, and the occasional extended bout of what I take to be K-Fed bitching – "Toy Soldier" ("I'm sick to death of toy soldiers! . . ./I'm so damn glad that's over") and the quite gorgeous Neptunes closer "Why Should I Be Sad?" with the Philly oasis which shimmers into view midsong contrasting pointedly with Spears' snarl at "stupid freaking things". But her closing invocation of "Time for me to move along" – which at one point provokes a semi-ironic "Hey baby, what's your name?" from Pharrell – and her "goodbye"s do not indicate a New Pop "Decades"; rather, the upstanding resignation of someone who throughout this record seems more firmly in control than on any of her previous ones; see for instance the hilarious Gwen Stefani send-up in the first verse of "Cool As Ice" (with curious "hooka hooka" backing vocals which seem to have strayed from Fleetwood Mac's *Tusk*).

For four, *Blackout* is so musically strong and packed with creamy nowness that most of the rest of this year's pop might as well get back into bed. When Britney does the schaffel schtick, as she does on "Radar" and "Ooh Baby Baby," we do not think of slumming Sloanes or Hoxtonites trying to pass themselves off as cutting edge but of rainbows old and horizons new – the repeated dove-like swoop of "on my radar" in the former might count as the greatest use of Autotune on record. Britney (and producer Farid Nassar) is even bold enough to revive the "Rock 'N' Roll Part 2" rhythm on the latter and make it sound like tomorrow; it is a not inconsiderable feat that I could easily imagine Elvis performing either tune.

But even if *Blackout* is not the apogee of nihilism that perhaps too many people were expecting – then again, neither was *In Utero* – it still has its "Be My Wife," its moment where everything suddenly clears and naked emotion is clarified, and "Heaven On Earth," the loveliest song that Britney has ever sung, is that moment. Its opening New Order-via-PSBs-via-Tiga sequencing bassline is promising enough but Spears – and Bloodshy & Avant – then build steadily on its foundations with more than a nod to Scritti's "Lions After Slumber" with its opening foray/seduction/catalogue of "Your touch, your taste, your breath, your face, your HANDS (Britney about to crumble at the prospect of those hands), you're sweet, your love, your teeth, your tongue, your eye (just one?), your mind, your lips, you're fine," intoned with breathless expectance of transformative ecstasy.

Then the melody begins to make itself known and there is some sharp intake of listener breath as one realizes how great and noble this song is going to be as the two-part chorus commences; the first, almost Motownish in a different world, bearing her already fainting "Waking up and you're next to me" with the emphasis floatingly on the "wake" and "next," the "look and you stop" leading to an abrupt pause, punctuated by an upwards squirting synth flourish, before the second part demonstrates such lyricism you want to cry all black holes into extinction via exhaustion – "when you're next to me it's just like heaven on earth" is not the most original of observations but in this setting carries the weight of paradises regained. The extended moment of the first half of the second verse – a slowly perambulating but determined "I'll move across the world for you," followed by "Just tell me when, just tell me where, I'll come to you" – is shattering, though immediately mended by the distant cry of a modified syndrum at 2:11.

The minor key piano echoes into view after the second chorus but it is laying down the foundations for happiness rather than digging an oblivion while synths detune, warp and chuckle behind. But even this does not prepare the listener for the "Strawberry Fields" citation which accompanies the "Fall off the edge of my mind" coda, after which words, for the first and final time on *Blackout*, fail her; "So in love," she mumbles in unreachable joy. "I said I'm so in love! With you!" she repeats as both voice and mind crack up ("Yeah!"). A brief electronic wave looms out of the distance before being cut off. The rest we'll have to guess, as Britney lets go.

19

John Stevens and Evan Parker: 23.40

8 November 2007

"We are the originators," says John Stevens, unambiguously and unapologetically, in his sleevenote to *The Longest Night*, the two-volume set of duet improvisations with Evan Parker recorded on 21 December 1976 (i.e. the longest night of the year) and released on Ogun, possibly that label's least typical release. No doubt in 1976 he felt it necessary to reiterate the importance of the music which the SME had enabled over the previous decade; a crucial facet of sixties musical utopia in imminent danger of being passed over or decried.

For an organiser of multiple collectives in multiple styles – at the same time as *The Longest Night*, he was appearing on the BBC's *Old Grey Whistle Test* as leader of the jazz-rock group John Stevens' Away – his mind was firmly his own and he expected his collaborators to bend to it, frequently with magnificent musical results, but with the equally frequent risk of fall outs and schisms. *The Longest Night* represented the first recorded intimate collaboration between the percussionist and the saxophonist in nearly a decade (though Parker appears, semi-anonymously, in the serried ranks of the Spontaneous Music Orchestra as heard on 1974's *SME = SMO* album; another of that ensemble's members, a young violin student named Stephen Luscombe, would a decade hence be a pop star as one half of Blancmange) – there had been serious aesthetic arguments, and Trevor Watts had tended to be Stevens' saxophonist of choice in his various groups.

So it's hardly surprising that these initial re-engagings should

by necessity be tentative. Much of the *Longest Night* material –
now reissued on CD, in combination with another duo session,
Corner To Corner, recorded in 1993, the year before Stevens'
death – comes across as delicate variations on the same theme;
fast but quiet interaction, Parker's soprano simultaneously more
percussive and more melodic than was his general 1976 wont,
twisting within the supple strings barely held together by
experience and intuition. Stevens confines himself to an
extremely minimalist kit, cymbals predominating over drums,
as though hiding in a cupboard to practice for fear of waking the
neighbors; yet he is quick to pick up on and refract Parker's
flurries and meditations. This kit's snare drum even came from
a children's set, and as though to emphasize the fact that
technical mastery alone wasn't what interaction and improvisation were all about, he occasionally picks up a cornet which he
similarly uses as an extra sheen of percussion.

The track titles, too, are utilitarian, detailing the start times of
each improvisation, but "23.40" which at ten and a half minutes
may safely be assumed to have been that night's final performance, is markedly different from its predecessors. It begins
with a lengthy drone which seems to be provided by Stevens'
voice while simultaneously blowing through his sans mouth-
piece, over which Parker improvises an unlikely devotional
pibroch. After two minutes there is a meaningful pause during
which Stevens settles with his percussion and he and Parker
bring some magical music into being. Ironically, given all the
standard pejoratives thrown at this music at the time –
including in my music class at school, to which I perhaps
unwisely brought the original *Vol 2* one afternoon ("the
strangest music I have ever heard in my life," my music teacher
remarked, "with the possible exception of Stockhausen." My
classmates responded as you might expect) – i.e. two drunks
turning over dustbins, squeaky mice evading crafty cats, etc.,
the aura of this music conjures up exactly those pictures. You

can easily imagine a starless, stoned limp through the midnight clothes lines of Cardiff terraced houses, or even, when Stevens fingers his finger cymbals and Parker blows on the edge of upper audibility, sexual congress. Fragments of melodic motifs appear on Parker's soprano and are carefully developed in tandem with the continued dialogue. At times Stevens seems to be rummaging through his kitchen cutlery drawer, at other times, particularly near the end, he ingeniously deploys his cymbals to form a root drone. Parker picks up on this instantly; loudness is the anti-issue in this form of improvised music, but a spark appears to be lit and he revs up towards his more typical circularities – Stevens' hi-hat dovetails immaculately, they reach a quick climax and then Parker gives a sardonic snort of a sign off; that was all very well, now let's get down to some serious stuff – there's still a lot of making up to be done.

20

Roy Harper: McGoohan's Blues

9 November 2007

1969's *Folkjokeopus* generally stands only moderately high in the critical pantheon of Roy Harper albums even though I can't think of too many other British folk or rock records of that period containing tracks dedicated to Albert Ayler ("One For All" – the young Harper befriended the great tenorman in his Copenhagen days, before *Spiritual Unity* and when he was still an on-off member of the Cecil Taylor Unit). And "McGoohan's Blues", all seventeen and a half minutes of it, deserves to be rescued from the backstream of indifference. The first of Harper's long-form pieces, it was quickly eclipsed by the more (in)famous "I Hate The White Man". And yet relative youth and naivety can sometimes provide deeper truths, having less to lose.

It's about a village by the seaside, and clearly an immediate post-war village ("The distant guns thunder my end"). Inspired to recollection by the sight of his young son asking him searching questions, he imagines his own youth and his would-be lover's youthful betrayal ("She weighed up the gains and the losses and, um, gave me the shove") and takes that as the triggering factor for an intentionally incontinent dream of the future a generation hence ...his village is not necessarily The Village, since that symbol is used for his great, shockingly passionate systematic denunciation of television, much of which still stands starkly relevant now ("Brainwashing innocent kids into thinking their way," "The Village TV hooks its victims with giveaway cash"), church hypocrisy ("As the world that Christ fought is supported by using his name"), the failure of the Welfare State ("I'm just a social experiment, tailored to slice"), even his own "fife-eyed promoter". It continues to pour, twenty years of quiet resentment spilling out into thrusting, endless guitar strokes, verse after verse – but Harper's delivery ensures the avoidance of didacticism since his voice is high, helpless, bewildered but also fearless; he aims for the most absurd of high notes in each chorus but keeps the listener utterly bound in his story, his parallel tale of the awkward individual ("Hmm ... insane") striding against the drift which society seems to insist on setting up for him and even against society itself if needs be – "... the system that keeps them in chains/Which is where they belong, with no poems, no love ... and no brains."

Although *The Prisoner* is repeatedly and subtly referenced ("the addicts are numbers who serve to perpetuate trash," "the luminous green prima donna is sniffing the sky"), "McGoohan's Blues" really represents Harper's own version of struggle against authority and how it spreads generously to suffocate any form of meaningful life if we are not careful. He concludes his anti-reverie with a chilling call, reflecting his original worry of "I've got no reply save to tell him it's all just a game," of "Well, there's nowhere to go, kid (i.e. if it isn't a joke), so you might as well start to freewheel." At this point his dream ends, and the original Rusholme ruffian is back with his Auntie Lily at the seaside town (as a war evacuee?), already knowing that his village – the one in which he was born and in which he will die (i.e. Britain) – is inescapable, just as "the ebb and the flow of the forces of life pass me by."

But it doesn't end here; he can't let it end here with his frightening yell of "To see all the dying lying ... **OBEYING!**"; he has to offer an alternative. So he stops playing the sequence he has been playing for the best part of twelve minutes, strums his acoustic more quietly (since the song has thus far been performed solo) and moves into a point of transition, brilliantly placing himself in the body of the weather balloon widely perceived as the enemy ... or a guard against one's baser self? "...an atom in a bubble on a wave that held its breath for one sweet second, then was popped and disappeared into fruitful futilities, meaningless meaning, meaningless meaning" ... and then he sticks on that last phrase in supra-falsetto baby talk (Rover as the womb?) ...

... and still no listener is prepared for the abrupt and shocking entry of the full band behind him as Harper unravels his ideal over ecstatically rolling piano and bass, a paradise of rainbows downstream, mountain fairgrounds, moonshine fountains and lemon tree blossom ladies pouring his tea (remember that the first voice we hear in the first episode of *The Prisoner*, some ten minutes in, is a tea shop waitress brightly reassuring Number 6 that "we'll be open in a minute" – is this an early notification of escape?), and it's all very "hello, Mike Scott". Harper grasps the real solution quickly: "And there's a mirror that I'm looking straight through – and I **GET** it!" and gladly sails or floats off to his "daffodil April" ("I'm floating to I don't know where!" he whispers gleefully), past "forests of restless chestmen, life is the same," as he leaves this wretchedly wronged world and his "stupid poetry" behind him – "And the fanfare I'm forcing through my teeth answers **NEVER!**" Alternatively he could be describing a curiously blissful apocalypse – the payoff line underlines the ambiguity. "The pumpkin coach and the rags approach/And the wind is devouring the ashes" – in other words, real life returns, the gloss and suppression and pretence discarded, and we have to learn to live with it and not click the door too soundly.

21

Insides: Walking In Straight Lines

14 November 2007

The first 30 seconds or so of this song suggest a microenvironment of possible future paths for pop forged from the best elements of the past and the (1993) present: "Sun Rising" delicately warped Deep House bass, Larry Heard rhythmic flutter, New Order untouched clangs, 1967 mellotron oscillations, Hank Marvin twangs and finally a fulsome beat. Singer/bassist Kirsty Yates intones the words like a particularly anxious Stevie Smith; epigrams indicating patience or dread. "Thanks for waiting. I'll start now. I'll walk over," giving nothing away. "Open-armed, with the widest smile [she plays three-dimensional chess with that "smile"] and the biggest heart, and suddenly I find myself led astray by wandering hands, excited thighs and thrilled nerve endings [that "endings" leading to the deepest of unfathomable breaths]." The music's volume never rises below mild but its matrix is persistent. "How long will I hold your attention? Would you wait another hour? A week? A year?" A pause. "Five years?" She reproaches herself ("Sounds to me like you have too much time on your hands") but continues, steadily and somewhat fearfully but knowing that turning back is not an option. "Still, thanks for waiting." Pause. "I'll start walking." Pause. "But I'll walk slowly."

At that "slowly" the electro pulse quickens up to double speed (although the beat remains at a constant midtempo). Her walk will last for what might seem like several consecutive lifetimes ... but she will reach there in the end because behind her lurks paralysis. Insides were a duo from Edinburgh and

Euphoria was the only album they ever made (before they mutated into Earwig and further from tangible reach); it hasn't survived on catalogue, but as an early somber female-centered counterpart to the subsequent amiably drunken quasi-shambles of Arab Strap (not to mention Lucky Pierre on a musical level) it's a future barely touched.

22

Nat "King" Cole: Unforgettable

2 December 2007

More than any other city, Toronto reminds me of Glasgow; a grid system of imperturbably long and straight streets guarded by imperious, high sandstone buildings. The streetcars also make me think of the old Glasgow trams on which my father briefly worked as a teenager to earn student holiday money. It looks older than its 200 or so years, and despite the surface appearance of prosperity in its centre its pockets of less than affluent areas very quickly become apparent. Nonetheless it was very reassuring to see the CN Tower blinking at us wherever we ventured, even from three or four miles away. As with the Post Office Tower (I can't get used to the BT Tower terminology) or St Paul's in London it is a reassuring beacon to remind us that we can never get lost in the city. At night it cascades into color; Tufty Club blue and yellow alternating with scarlet and green. However, even after a few days back in London it is also apparent that Toronto is a far politer city. Try putting your left hand up when crossing the road to stop a car in London and see how many emergency operations you'll need in hospital. The people, even to an extent the thrusting Mulroneykids, seem less in a rush, less prevailed upon (usually by themselves) to project An Image.

With expert timing (ha!) I flew into Toronto in the immediate aftermath of their heaviest snowfall in months. As the 'plane descended through the clouds the outlying suburb of Scarborough was white and unpeopled, and we spent a tricky half hour inching our way along the marathon runways at

Pearson Airport since they were covered by sheer ice. Meanwhile the slush of the city streets was already freezing over, and Lena and I had to pick our way through treacherous blocks with heavy luggage. Still, when we checked in at the Baldwin Village Inn (which I thoroughly recommend to all Toronto-visiting readers, particularly those with a penchant for the writings of Margaret Atwood and Michael Ondaatje), it suddenly felt like Christmas. We crept next door to the Vegetarian Haven restaurant, which was, shall we say, functional but protein-friendly – however it did not matter because we were together again and so utterly happy.

Other memories are plentiful. The brass band in Nathan Phillips Square on Friday morning playing Bachman-Turner Overdrive's "Takin' Care Of Business" in the style of the Brotherhood of Breath; the resonant, name-encrypting bells of the Cathedral Church of St James which I had waited a long time to hear and feel; McTamney's the jewellers in Church Street for the quality and *humanity* which the diamond-heavy likes of People's Jewellers will never understand; the house dog who kept sneezing on our feet; a glorious Sunday wandering out into Queen St West, taking in the fantastic Pages bookshop where I picked up a much desired (and totally unavailable in Britain) book, *Secret Carnival Workers* by Paul Haines, leading to Rotate This! Records – Toronto's answer to Rough Trade – where as we entered, Kevin Drew and Brendan Canning were leaving; we were too starstruck to ask them useful questions, e.g. playing at our London wedding ceremony – and Chippy's, indisputably the world's greatest indie fish and chip shop; as we came in "I Wanna Be Your Dog" was blasting out over the speakers, and as we sat contentedly munching our gigantic haddock and cod packages the Lullabye Arkestra album was played in its ecstatically epileptic entirety (we only found out who they were after Lena asked for an artist ID; needless to say we rushed immediately back to Rotate This! to pick up a copy, and of course it was the last copy they had in the shop); the extensive and quite alarming Sonic Boom second hand record shop at Bloor Street W, massive and perhaps intimidatingly so, even though they have perhaps the best used cassette section I've ever seen outside of Brighton, and I randomly found the long sought *Mary Queen Of Scots* CD by Eugenius for Lena; the humbly lovely Kensington Market and the Big Fat Burrito Cafe, the best indie burrito cafe you're likely to see . . .

There are many other deeply personal memories too but nothing can surpass Saturday, 24 November, when we became husband and wife before 25 or so close friends and family members in the "party room" downstairs in the apartment block where Lena lives – the minister was beyond fantastic, the food (lovingly and untiringly prepared by my mother in law and her team) wonderful, and the music uncanny, spot on and fabulous, able to encompass both "Party Fears Two" and "Dancing Queen" (air piano ahoy!), Monk's "Misterioso" (yes!) and "Get Ur Freak On."

And, of course, "Unforgettable," which was our first dance; recently resurrected by Nas for the brilliant "Can't Forget About You," that rarest of phenomena, a rap record about contentment, stability and positive memory – but for our first dance it had to be the original; smooth, heartfelt, lush, deep, pleasantly astonished and utterly dedicated and truthful. And so, six years after thinking that I'd never experience this situation again, I am once again married and completely in love, have returned to a new home in London (which by the current look of the front room will take two months to sort out/unpack, but hey, that's the fun and purpose of it) and – well, I've returned to the life I used to have, except now it is new and even more glorious.

23

Kylie Minogue: Wow

3 December 2007

There is an eerily familiar tendency to berate Kylie (softly, with the brushed end of a broomstick) over the head for not returning with a concept album about cancer and betrayal unlike SHOCK-INGLY AWARE, PRO-ACTIVE Britney who is ON THE SUSPECT CASE with her ACUTE GRASP of her not-remotely-resembling-Kelly-Rowland (but oddly-resembling-Kevin-Rowland) dilemma. Not that I want to demur on behalf of *Blackout* which as a pop album the rest of the century will find hard to surpass; it is beyond great and its awareness and grasp do not require mandatory capitalisation. But if Kylie wants to come back from what she was thrust into with an album of more-complicated-than-we-seem dancefloor sexpop then I'm likewise happy about that. Then again, this *X* album of hers is not bereft of demons; it bears the most disturbing front/back cover of any record since Simon Finn's *Pass The Distance* – the awkwardly candid eyebrow raising amidst the white and red polkadots on the front contrasting with the nightmare negative image on the reverse; is it Mephistopheles' butterfly, an image of her own expiry?

The muted critical reception – other than the standard picture of men wanting Kylie to suffer on their behalf – is pretty inexplicable since *X* sounds mostly terrific (in 1981 terms, it's a sort of Olivia Newton-John to *Blackout*'s Kim Wilde). This is made particularly explicit by the two Bloodshy and Avant contributions which sound worldly yet suitably unworldly. "Speakerphone" is mellifluously desperate to be human, and

"Nu-Di-Ty" padlocks Gwen S's trunk for good with its unprecedented Cabaret Voltaire/Roswell Rudd interface. "Into Your Arms" is sparky enough to make one temporarily forgive Calvin Harris. "2 Hearts" makes a better rockist fist than the overly prosaic rock (Brighton or Budgie?) of the new Girls Aloud platter. And I will leave it to others to extol to the important stars "The One," another song which I wish Billy MacKenzie had survived long enough to hear or sing with its exquisite Miro float of a chorus ("Loveme loveme loveme LOVE ME!") and its never more apt story ("I'm the one!," "I'm connecting with you," "Are you receiving me?").

For here I will reserve unalloyed love for "Wow," the record's most straightforward (although it is hardly straightforward) pop/dance song and the one which, when she performed it on The *Kylie Show*, I initially mistook for Special Guest Star G Stefani before realizing there was no such thing. Another miraculous production from Greg Kurstin – when are people going to recognize the unassuming genius of this man, LA's own Brian Higgins? – "Wow"'s central motif of processed mouths-as-muted-plunger-trombone-section ("WowWowWowWOW!") seems to construct a daisy chain of all great girl pop right back to the Boswells and the Andrews and its early 1982 purple glow is smashing, with its "Look Of Love"/"Holiday" chord sequence (but its 2007 rhythms!) and its subject matter of dancing, and looking, and fancying, and taking it from here (no more Glums, or as another track has it "No More Rain"); "I Should Be So Lucky"'s necessary bookend, the melting, poised icicle of the "Every inch of you smells of desire" section of the chorus. She's lucky that she can sing this, we're luckier that we can dance and love to it, and the car drives on ("You're such a rush! The rush is never ending!") so let's enjoy the newly green city in full knowledge of the highway we had to dream to reach there. You got it? XXXX!

The Zombies: The Way I Feel Inside

4 December 2007

It is the first track on our wedding CD and the only one of its eighteen tracks which doesn't date from 1967. It originally stole in, unnoticed, towards the end of 1966 as the B-side of their flop single "Gotta Get A Hold Of Myself". Even by 1966 standards it's a startling construct; Colin Blunstone strolls unhurriedly through the echoing studio corridors, approaches the microphone, takes a preparatory breath and sings quietly, and slightly fearfully, about what he feels and whether she feels the same way too and is it just possible that she might and if so but how will he know and he'll just have to keep it to himself until he knows for sure. Some considerable distance is implied by the resonance of Blunstone's voice set against and blending into the natural resonance of the recording studio itself; although the vocal line itself only suggests the rich harmonic structure of the underlying song, the melody is cleverly constructed so that the echoes supply their own bedrock of a cathedral – and this was some time before Alvin Lucier sat in that room, different to the one we are in now.

Eventually Rod Argent joins in on organ, and later adding the bass pedals, but it still doesn't feel as though the full song has been revealed; Blunstone's unaffected poignancy is quietly devastating – he wants her so much, can barely hope to breathe without wanting (her) to say something, but for now he can only hold it in, and hope. And abruptly, the piece ends; Blunstone drops a penny which we can hear whirling onto the floor, in anticipation of her finding it and placing it in her shoe, and shuffles out of the studio. He doesn't know (yet), so we only receive part of the picture of the song, rather than all of it in its full and proud flourish – but we know how badly he wants to sing it, unleashed and fulfilled. And despite his hesitancy of delivery, there is a quiet and humble confidence that he will eventually be given the chance to speak. With that as a prelude you can see how magnificently something like Blunstone's 1974 "Wonderful"/"Beginning"/"Keep The Curtains Closed Today" trilogy acts as a gesture of liberation and consolidation of confirmed mutual love. But of course it also acts as a suitable prelude to our own story, and the rest of the tracklisting should hopefully be sufficient without my needing to sketch it out further. Anyway, in response to multiple requests, the eighteen tracks on our wedding CD were as follows:

1. The Zombies – The Way I Feel Inside (if only. . .)
2. The Turtles – Happy Together (wouldn't it be nice?)
3. The Marvelettes – The Hunter Gets Captured By The Game (my God, he feels the same and I didn't know!)
4. The Monkees – I'm A Believer (beginning of our time)
5. The Spencer Davis Group – I'm A Man (no longer a prisoner of the past)
6. The Mamas and The Papas – Dedicated To The One I Love (the darkest hour is just before dawn)
7. The Lovin' Spoonful – Darlin' Be Home Soon (relief!)
8. Marvin Gaye and Tammi Terrell – Ain't No Mountain High Enough (it only takes eight hours)
9. The Association – Windy (bending down to give me a rainbow)
10. Smokey Robinson and The Miracles – More Love (the first major Motown side cut in LA and suddenly the breathing is easier; the intro itself is responsible for inventing everything from Westbrook's "Original Peter" to Charles and Eddie's "Would I Lie To You"? – and yes, more love, better

love, realer love. . .)

11. The Byrds – Have You Seen Her Face? (dazed but ecstatic)

12. Stevie Wonder – I Was Made To Love Her ("My baby NEEDS me!" No longer kept inside)

13. Pink Floyd – See Emily Play (the only way is UP. . .)

14. The 13th Floor Elevators – Slip Inside This House (. . .and UP. . .)

15. Scott Walker – Montague Terrace (In Blue) (the world continues its winding way but we are HAPPY because we KNOW. . .)

16. Aretha Franklin – (You Make Me Feel Like A) Natural Woman (wowwowwowWOW. . .)

17. Love – You Set The Scene (Arthur thought he was dying when he wrote and recorded this and he wasn't – not just yet anyway – but heavens, that "oh-wowowowowowWOW . . ." and it is now OUR time and that's sweet . . .)

18. The Beach Boys - Darlin' (Brian getting back from the brink, rediscovering simplicity and joy and happiness – a more than fitting upbeat finale and a happy ending!)

25

Was (Not Was) Starring Mel Torme: Zaz Turned Blue

7 December 2007

If you think you owe somebody one, don't be surprised if they bend you out of your way for the payback. David Was gave Mel Tormé a rave review sometime in 1982; Tormé got in touch and suggested working together. I'm not sure how much attention he devoted to the lyrics on the first Was (Not Was) album but those on the second, *Born To Laugh At Tornadoes*, were sufficiently warped to darn at least one of Paul Haines' socks. The album has never appeared on CD; some say this was down to Tormé's reticence to let the world hear "Zaz Turned Blue," but the track did appear carefully hidden away at the tail end of a posthumous 4CD box set.

The key is that Tormé sings it straight. The song is a light-verging-on-terminal vignette, perched midway between Carver and Coupland, about this kid Zaz who indulges with wrestling-hold-as-psychoasphyxiation-turn-on one night in the park ("Steve squeezed his neck/He figured ... what the heck?") but then collapses ("Zaz turned blue ... what were we supposed to do?") following which he joins the Marines – "at the age of eighteen" Tormé intones with Tom Clay-ish solemnity – fights, or maybe doesn't fight, for a bit, then comes back to hang out, shoot pool and wear a silly grin on his chin. A typical Was (Not Was) scenario, in other words.

But Tormé and his pianist Mike Renzi don't treat it like chapter 439 of "Out Come The Freaks". The Velvet Fog applies his most tender compassion to the song, treats it as though it were "It Was A Very Good Year" or "None But The Lonely Heart"; his tenor soft, tactile, arching to noble when required, the melody played slowly and delicately. With his final, undemonstrably extended "blue," into which he indeed seems to vanish into the blue of the air, Tormé turns the song into a starkly lush elegia; for what, it's not quite certain, but he defies both himself and his listener to drop the straight face. He clearly had some idea of the cumulative absurdity of what he was singing, and in turn what does that tell us about Pavlovian responses to emotional signifiers related to the grain of a voice? He started out in 1946 as one of Artie Shaw's bluffingly bright harmony singers wondering "What Is This Thing Called Love?" and in the intermediate lifetime he continually sought to supersede the notion of voice as direct expression of words; he was Art Pepper without the horn and without the drug hassles. "Zaz Turned Blue"'s implication might yet turn out to be: was that all there was?

26

The Faces: You Can Make Me Dance, Sing Or Anything (Even Take The Dog For A Walk, Mend A Fuse, Fold Away The Ironing Board Or Any Other Domestic Shortcomings)

11 December 2007

It was their last word, though was never strictly intended to be; caught up in the Christmas rush it peaked at #12 in our charts at the end of 1974, and in America it charted not at all. But "You Can Make Me Dance, Sing Or Anything. . ." still sounds like the most gracious and good-natured of musical farewells, and certainly marks the last audible occasion when Rod sounded as though he was enjoying making a record rather than clocking in to make one. The band's shared composer credits suggest an impromptu jam slowly shaping its way into a song, and the ebullience and spark of both playing and singing betray a group playing together and loving it.

Rod offers the reliable old lyrical raincoat of yes baby, I know I'm an irretrievably recidivist, womanizing sot, but hey I always bring it on home to you; a scenario you would hardly accept from the subsequent Atlantic-crossing, tax-dodging solo Stewart but here his frequent exclamations of "ooh baby!" and the best "listen!"s this side of Kevin Rowland keep our sympathy afloat. "You can make me do just any old thing!" he proclaims in the chorus, and follows with the winking aside ". . . and I love it." He knows that summer will merge into winter and he'll never learn a thing, but "this old heart of mine" – he leaps at the paraphrase – "is far too proud not to keep on trying" and besides "I'd rather LOSE BOTH MY eyes/Than never see your smiling face again, girl."

Beside and behind him the band cook up most agreeably. Ian MacLagan's funky post-Stevie clavinet (and discreet Hammond asides) squirting in symmetry with Ronnie Wood's deadpan guitar responses to Rod's latest apology/justification, although the star here is Kenney Jones, thudding a definite foursquare beat on snare and floor tom as though this is his last chance to beat the beat. But the miracle of the song comes with the final turnaround; as Stewart murmurs "Keep on lovin' me baby" and the record appears to be reaching a natural quietude of an end, the key suddenly changes upward and late hope comes flooding in through the scratched French windows; refueled, Stewart plays with the words "baby" and "darling," reveling in their implications as the band eagerly make their final push – the punctum coming with Jones' gavel-like quartet of cymbal/snare splashes/crashes answering Rod's four ascending "darling"s (who'd have thought the influence of Levon Helm would stretch so far?) and an unobtrusive string section enters with Oriental curlicues to take the record, and the band, out on the highest of highs. Nine months later, Rod was sailing and lost to wonder forever.

27

American Music Club: Last Harbor

12 December 2007

California still seems to me the unequivocal masterpiece in the American Music Club/Mark Eitzel canon: an opaque reflection on betrayal, isolation and love lost and rediscovered which defies the boundary of existence/non-existence by degrees daring by even 1988 (*Spirit Of Eden*/69) standards, and its long-term absence from circulation – caused by our old friend, Legal Issues – remains regrettable. Eitzel sometimes appears to defy happiness through crying on the soft, graying outwards sands of *California* – hear his collapse on the final "Jenny don't go" on the song "Jenny" – but "Last Harbor" signals either a last wave before slow drowning or the slower realization of a gradual dawn.

He starts the song sounding as beaten as any male singer I can think of, over a bare background of mid-tempo mid-register acoustic guitar and discreet bass, meditating on the many faces of betrayal and false new starts: "Some of them are kind and it's phony/Some of them are kind . . . and it's OK . . ." but he's losing his spiritual grip. "Falling, falling," he falls before exclaiming in slow-motion horror, "Hey, I can't see the bottom!," his "bottom" bottoming out in the faint hope that it might act as parachute, before climbing to Art Garfunkel heights – tonally unsteady, but totally heartfelt – to ask "are you gonna be my last harbor?"

Then he laughs-cum-sobs the second verse, perhaps to mock, or more urgently to convince himself: "She'll soon find a way to make you feel fine/She's laughing and she's clapping her hands/As she walks across your cup of wine" – note the ambiguous Biblical reference – "She'll make it real easy for you," he sings with slightly more strength, before falling in a float through the distended syllables of "all you've got to do is remember her name" and landing on a stern "She's almost your passport to the world" followed by a slightly breathless and expectant "She's almost your ticket out . . . again!" as though he cannot quite believe in himself that she is the actual answer.

The chorus is sung once more, and then, after a pause to allow a presumed answer, he repeats the "are you gonna be . . . my . . . last . . .har. . .bor?" question more hoarsely, more vulnerably, more life-saving pleadingly descending in scale until that "bor" finds its buoy in a sudden, subtle Pacific Ocean horizon of distant synthesizer (thus underlining the parallel with Dennis Wilson's *Pacific Ocean Blue*, especially "Thoughts Of You"). Eitzel reiterates the first two lines of the first verse while the synth implies but doesn't fanfare a resolving major chord, before quietly concluding: "Some of them never tell you/Just how much they'll give away," with which he merges with both sea and sky as guitar and bass fade into the middleground as the synth turns everything into a transcendent gasp of quiet wonder until it becomes a Whistler blur of beauty; not so much the last harbor before expiration but the patient rising of a new sun, and spiritually not that far away from the Spanish quays of AR Kane; swimming with strokes generous.

28

Van Morrison: Come Here My Love

13 December 2007

He has a slightly scared look on his face, there on the cover of *Veedon Fleece*, even though he looks to be protected in the middle of not quite utterable peace. Is he afraid those Irish wolfhounds might turn on him? Should his distant resemblance to Nick Drake in this picture, taken in late 1974, cause concern? An abandoned cigarette, a groove-worn second side of a blues album from 1958 which doesn't cut like it used to, the glass half-expectant; his voice booms out the title with Cyril Cusack authority but no one is even looking for hardness here: "This feeling has me spellbound/Yet the storyline, in paragraphs, laid down the same." Once again, it is voice and guitar only, sitting in a room different to the one his love is in now. "I'm mystified - OH! - by this mood," (that "OH!" as though he'd had a nanosecond of revelatory vision; piece them all together and would they listen?) "This melancholy feeling that just don't do no good" – the way he always slides into those Skip James elisions when life is at stake (cf. "Slim Slow Slider," the leaves which fall all the way down side one of *Hard Nose The Highway*) – he is unsure whether to prolong existence but will make the effort: "Come here my love/And I will lift my spirits high for you," he pledges in a less resonant, more intimate baritone, but where flamingos fly so do Gil Evans and Jimmy Knepper and his scarred memories. "I'd like to fly away and spend a day or two/Just contemplating the fields and leaves and talking about nothing," and talks that "nothing" as though it is "everything" which of course it is and then the Joycean global scan of "shades of effervescent, effervescent odors/and shades of time and tide" flowing through towards an innate understanding of and communion with the "intrigue of nature's beauty," a forest, a globe visualised in her shining eyes. Finally he is nearly unable to speak because of wonder: "Come along with me/and take it all in" – he entreats, he pleads – "come here, my love." Rochester melting and becoming himself before Jane, but then you guessed that already. He knows there's no need to be scared.

29

Mott The Hoople: Ballad Of Mott
(March 26th 1972 Zurich)

3 January 2008

"I changed my name in search of fame/To find the Midas touch."

The song sits oddly on an album which is generally upbeat musically, if more qualified lyrically - 1973's *Mott* - as Ian Hunter looks back, over gentle needlestick waves of acoustic guitar and unhurried ventilation shafts of rhythm, at a time when he nearly had to break up the band. As an allegorical anthem for thwarted ambition it is far more convincing and affecting than "American Pie," since it is the precise obverse of "All The Young Dudes" and also because it is a song whose composer brooks no regret, even as he addresses the fourth wall ("You know the band so well/Still I feel, somehow, we let you down"). He spits out polite contempt at the spectacle of the "rock 'n' roll circus," itemizing the loss of "childlike dreams" and the pointlessness of being "just a rock 'n' roll star" at a point (March 1972) when stardom still seemed far from their grasp.

"We went off somewhere on the way/And now I see we have to pay"

Somewhere the singer knows, or thinks he knows, that he has taken a wrong turning, but it's the scorpion astride the frog once more; he'll sting, they'll both drown, but it's his nature: "Oh but if I had my time again/You all know just what I'd do," because as deflating and perhaps as willfully suicidal as the spectacle and practice may seem, it mesmerizes, and Hunter can't get the notion of the greater good out of his mind or his heart. He has to carry on, and clings to those final, extended, quivering "miiii-iiiind"s like tentacles of pure cord. Sometimes he's right, sometimes he just gets lost in routine disruptions – as *Diary Of A Rock 'N' Roll Star* quietly illustrates, there was a fiery resentment heating up beneath those shades of fading visions – so he won't erase the final vision, the concept of rock 'n' roll being more than its sum parts, something that can change worlds where other forms of showbiz, including politics, couldn't. Does he imply that he'd die for his vision to be preserved? Does purity of vision necessarily presuppose emotional constancy or the absence of internal conflicts? It's impossible to tell, but the purpose isn't, whatever its origins and whatever its eventual end; and so I think of this Ballad and the erstwhile President of the Mott the Hoople Fan Club and alumnus of Lady Margaret Hall, Oxford, Benazir Bhutto, who died over Christmas for the alleged sin of wanting twice as much.

30

Barry Manilow: Could It Be Magic?

4 January 2008

Following the predictable but agreeable strains of Aly's fiddle and Phil's accordion on BBC1 Scotland's *Hogmanay Show*, a timeworn ritual marred only by a hoarse Marti Pellow slaughtering some hapless auld folk song, and with a view to avoiding the Soul, Passion and Honesty of *Jools Holland's Mid-November Hootenanny* – despite its supposedly stellar cast list, Ruby Turner seemed to be belching away every time I flicked over to BBC2 – I turned over for reassurance, or refuge, to the Take That O2 Arena concert, broadcast on Scottish TV about half an hour after it took place. My mum loves the jigs and reels of Messrs Bain and Cunningham but loved Take That even more, and I could see her point. It set me thinking just how great an album an imagined combination of *Beautiful World* and Robbie Williams' *Rudebox* might have been – in the White Album sense – with Gary's staunch reliability counterbalancing Robbie's rambles. Occupying a midspace pitched between the Pet Shop Boys at Wembley '91, *Close Encounters* and Torvill And Dean's *Holiday On Ice*, the performance proved that Take That had learned from New Pop in terms of presentation if not quite in terms of music. The deployment of Cee-Lo Green – in the Lulu role on "Relight My Fire" (into which he interspersed a snatch of "Crazy") and as general wise seer and handyman elsewhere – was certainly a coup though I hope that Green doesn't get cul-de-sacked into having to find even more novel and exhausting ways of singing that one song on tap, since his *Cee-Lo Green ... Is The Soul Machine* has slowly increased in attraction over the last few years and may well end up one of this decade's key albums.

The keystone, though, was "Could It Be Magic," which Take That now interpret in the original Manilow arrangement. Taken in tandem with the subtle lyric change in "Never Forget" (now it's "and we're not so young"), the performance illustrated the strangely logical duality of youth and adult responses to pop; back in early 1993 they sped it up even faster than Donna Summer managed and delivered the song in a boisterous hi-NRG (moderate setting) manner. And of course, Robbie sang the original lead; one still can't visualize him doing so now, and certainly not in this environment. So the band had to retrench and reconsider – and it came out as a performance of no small wonder.

Manilow's original – released on album in 1975, a US hit single in 1976 and eventually a UK hit single in 1979 (in Britain, Manilow has always been viewed and adored as a live act and as an albums artist, in that order) – still strikes me as one of the last expressions of the 1967-8 move towards avant-balladry (*Scott 3, Odessa, A Tramp Shining* etc.); long and in its own boldly modest way experimental, which begins and ends the same but not in the same place. One can imagine "Could It Be Magic?" as the dream of the young Julliard student, brushing up on his Chopin at the library piano; the song is based on Chopin's Prelude in C Minor (Op 28, No 20 to be exact), a piece very familiar to me in early 1979 since I had to learn it as part of my Grade V piano lessons. He drifts into abstractly suppressed pleas for inspiration ("Spirits move me") but then with carefully gradated passion expresses his joy and wonder at the woman he loves and who seems to love him. I have no idea whether his "sweet Melissa" (diplomatically changed by Gary Barlow to "you're my lifeline") was fellow Arista recording artist Melissa Manchester, but he is clearly spellbound, tentatively making his way up the arching stairway of "Baby I love you" before strings echo his yearning request – "Come, come, come into my arms"

– and underscore his bewildered but already bordering on ecstatic rhetorical question of "Could this be the magic at last?"

His tentativeness of delivery also excuses the occasional odd lyrical lapse – shouldn't she be the "answer to all questions I can find" rather than the "answer to all answers," and I'm not quite sure of the extra-astrological significance of the point where the stallions meet the sun; it all fits with the song's emotional tenor, however, and note how the bass sighs as Manilow makes his key push towards enlightenment and union, answered by sliding cymbal and middleground choir – the procession is so natural sounding that I don't at all mind the clear orchestra cues of his spoken "Come on!"s, since it continues to build up with true boldness until drums crash, hands clap en masse (the specter of Spector isn't far away: cf. Dion's "Make The Woman Love Me," recorded the same year) and Barry's "**COME!**"s reveal their true meaning; poignant because the song never quite shifts out of the minor key, and therefore out of uncertainty. It climaxes with the repeated fanfares (they've come) of the French horns upon which Manilow's voice disappears into the ether of oneness, leaving the post-"Hey Jude" arrangement to continue, possibly forever and putting me in mind of the pivotal role of the French horn as emotional catalyst in pop – think of, inter alia, First Class' "Beach Baby," Nancy Sinatra's "You Only Live Twice" (the Hazlewood-produced version) and Billy Fury's "In Thoughts Of You" – before that phantasm, that splendid chimera, also vanishes, leaving Barry alone again, at the piano, bringing the Prelude to a close with the huge question mark of his final two chords, i.e. will it happen, and if so is it magic? One 1979 Sunday afternoon, on the Top 40 countdown, it was followed by "The Staircase (Mystery)" by Siouxsie and the Banshees – another great single in one of our greatest years for singles – and nobody understood how or why I could be bewitched by both, or indeed either. But the song's naïvely knowing greatness has endured, perhaps most greatly in the version sung by Sylvester and his keyboard player Eric Robinson on the *Living Proof* album, recorded live at the San Francisco Opera House at around the same time as half of a medley with Leon Russell's "A Song For You" – the two turn it into a hymn of holy devotion, and their final, extended beyond all rational forms of breath, declaration of the "last" on "could this be the magic at last?" are like Isis and Osiris arising from their golden slumbers to the bluest air of transcendence and peace.

31

Dion: Born To Be With You

11 January 2008

Although the orchestra which surrounded Dion and Spector in 1975 was as large as ever – and with nine guitarists, two bassists and three drummers *inter alia* it was arguably larger than it had been a decade previously – their "Born To Be With You" sounds anything but opulent. It is as though a blind had been turned upwards and the light of day finally permitted to shine its attempted luster upon the Wall. Released as an uncut single ahead of the album, running for over six minutes, Sean Rowley recalls in his sleevenote to the CD reissue of *Born To Be With You* his awestruck fourteen-year-old self, listening to the late Roger Scott's Capital Radio drivetime show, home from school, ear glued to transistor, with Scott playing the track twice consecutively and warning the listener that "this record will change your life". Up in Glasgow, we had to make do with Radio Clyde (though its evening programming was infinitely more adventurous and varied than you'd expect) and so I had to rely on an *NME* rave review to persuade my dad to buy the single, released on the shortlived Phil Spector International imprint; the album hardly appeared in the shops and I didn't hear it or even come across a copy until many years later. The single was not a hit on either side of the Atlantic and has yet to be noticeably revived on oldies radio.

Everyone who has heard it agrees that it should have been a massive hit, but it may be that its intrinsic elements militated against anything approaching success, not to mention the British climate of the time; the singles chart of 1975 was so qualitatively lopsided that even Springsteen's "Born To Run" (and both Bruce and Miami Steve dropped into the Born To Be With You sessions to watch their idols at work) failed to penetrate our Top 50 filled with workaday novelties, folk singers turned comedians, glutinous MoR and AoR, inexplicable reissues and pallid post-glam teenpop (it was an exceptional year for black [and black influenced] dance music and reggae, but again that was only partially reflected in the year's lists).

Then again, Dave Edmunds' more vigorous, uptempo Spectorish take on the same song had gone top ten in Britain two years previously, and it is likely that the Dion/Spector "Born To Be With You" sports its cloak of greatness in anticipation of its expected failure. Bobby Gillespie has likened the record's aura to a New Orleans funeral but the great, elephantine push and pull of the mass of players, determinedly weighing the song downwards, makes it seem far older; I think of the horses struggling to pull Queen Victoria's coffin at the turn of the last century.

And yet, Dion manages, indeed does his superhuman best, to shine above this sepulchral procession; the ensemble is clumsier than Spector would have allowed in '65 but also more human – witness Frank Capp accidentally dropping a cymbal a third of the way through the long instrumental intro amidst the crawling cathedral of slide guitars as Jew's harps, sludge containers of drums. Nino Tempo was given the tenor sax obbligatos and he too rises above the seeming mourning in a valiant attempt to escalate and magnify renewed or revealed light.

Meanwhile, Dion himself remains utterly noble, easily leaping towards confidently capturing high notes and holding them, scatting against Nino's runs, sounding as pure as any 1956 mother could have wanted "rock 'n' roll" to have sounded, even sacred – his seemingly throwaway "Sleep eternally" is the key to the record; it is almost as though he is twirling the baton reluctantly at the head of the cortege, manfully resisting the urge to pull a bugle out of his concealed jacket pocket and go into "Oh, Didn't He Ramble?" And yet the song is one of consecrated confirmation of love, faith and devotion, and Dion lends it all the worship it deserves, and more besides, as strings scrub in the same not-quite-distinct middleground. Eventually he attains catharsis, and his final "uh!" seems like a confirmed vow as he cheerfully trades fours with Nino towards the slowest of fades. The record comes across as the missing link between Bing Crosby and Gorecki; to be worshipped and prayed towards, if not to be bought and beatified at home.

32

Reparata: Shoes

15 January 2008

The bouzouki doesn't feature much in seventies pop except when it has to (e.g. some of Demis Roussos' hits, Barry Ryan's "Red Man" or one-offs like Iannis Markopoulos' theme tune to the BBC drama series *Who Pays The Ferryman?*); the main exception is Barry Blue who used the device successfully, if briefly, on "Dancin' On A Saturday Night" and, less sanely (no bad thing), on "Hot Shot". I can't find any parallel for "Shoes," however; it floated inexplicably into the lower regions of both UK and US charts towards the end of 1975. Prior to that Reparata was known as the frontwoman of Brooklyn's Reparata and the Delrons, one of the most underestimated of sixties girl groups; over here they had just the one hit with the Kenny Young-penned "Captain Of Your Ship," top 20 in 1968 and a clear antecedent to Noosha Fox with its extended bar-leaping sighs and nautical double entendres. In America their best was #60 in 1964 with "Whenever A Teenager Cries". They ran the expected girl group evolutionary gamut with great aesthetic, if not commercial, success; 1966's Jeff Barry-penned "I'm Nobody's Baby Now" is one of the best of all counterfeit Spector records and 1968's extraordinary "Saturday Didn't Happen," which Suzi Quatro has rightly pinpointed as where the Shangri-Las might have gone had they lasted long enough to tackle psychedelia.

But "Shoes" is something else; electro-klezmer? *My Big Pre-ZE Records Greek Wedding*? Not quite Eurodance (in the 1975 "Una Paloma Blanca"/"El Bimbo" sense) but not quite shaking off psychedelia while at the same time partly anticipating gay disco, Reparata sings of Johnny and Louise, getting married, seeing Papa smile, avoiding maternal abuse by remembering the bride's shoes and so forth; it is possibly the last pop record to use the term "gay" in its original sense ("Everything's so grand and gay/We can frolic all day"), and yet despite the surface bonhomie the music's thrust is slightly threatening and more than slightly unreal, particularly in the middle section when the beat cuts out to let through an ethereal cloud of disheveled angel choirs – not quite Kander and Ebb, only nearly Jobriath – while Reparata's voice strolls as serenely as Carole Bayer Sager's though cannot dispel the feeling that something isn't quite right with the scenario. As indeed it turned out not to be; a fellow Delron had by then become one of Barry Manilow's backing singers and put it about that she was the "real Reparata"; the ensuing legal battle, which dragged on for some years, ensured that Reparata herself could not promote "Shoes" and thus the single wasn't as big as it might have been. Still, its strangeness is a direct precedent of things like Cristina's "Is That All There Is?" without ever being as explicit. The glasses remain poised in the air, never to be smashed.

33

Patsy Ann Noble: I Did Nothing Wrong

24 January 2008

She came from Australia, and as the actress Trisha Noble eventually returned there, via the States, but in the mid-sixties tried her luck as a pop singer in Britain without notable success; "I Did Nothing Wrong" suggests we may have missed out. She appeared in an episode of *Danger Man* set entirely on an abandoned oil rig, rigged up as a pirate radio station, and her "He Who Rides A Tiger" – which, *pace* Wikipedia, was not a hit – and "I Did Nothing Wrong," recorded and released in 1964, carries the lurid and rather disturbing hyperreality which tended to arise from McGoohan's sundry worlds.

The model is anxious Cilla Black, but the backing is unusually sharp and more than a little hostile; the organ pierces, the drums slash crisply across the already damaged canvas. If Cilla had been permitted to record "Love Of The Loved" with the proto-punk backing band she had in the Cavern this is how that may have sounded. Noble plays the part of a girl who has apparently been caught out, and is at rather too anxious pains to deny any symptoms of infidelity – "We only took a walk/And all we did was talk"; "He only came to me/For friendly sympathy – but note how her voice shudders on that "came" like an imaginary knife being held at her throat.

She tries to overturn all indicators of denial by sheer pleading force – "How could I hold you now . . ./If I had held another boy last night?" – but becomes slightly over-defensive when she asserts that "You know I love you so/And [you are] smart enough to know/In whose arms I belong" as though trying to salvage whatever she can from the veracity, or otherwise, of her tale; the implication being is that she's done something more, and thus the emphasis of the title becomes heavier with every breath, as does the avalanche of Hammond and Selmer behind her, until she pierces a scream of "Believe me baby!" and four terrible hammer blows of "no" – she is close to collapse on the third – before the song grinds to its baleful and disturbing end. It is exactly the sort of pastiche pop song which would have played in the Village; too primary colored to be genuine, too hysterical to be palpable, the scream of static when pillows are pushed against the speakers to try to muffle them, even if you imagine that Number 6 would have been driven to far greater distraction by non-stop Doonican and Bachelors. An intensity only approached in sixties non-charting Brit girl pop by Tammy St John, and a record in which, perhaps not ironically, she has to struggle to retain nobility. An astonishing listen, but I'm more than glad that the world has moved on since then.

34

Billy Fury: Run To My Loving Arms

29 January 2008

This week marks the twenty-fifth anniversary of Billy Fury's passing; a quarter of a century since his prematurely weary heart finally gave out, barely into his forties and on the verge of what might have been an exceptionally remarkable comeback. The danger of over-romanticizing is already abundantly clear, but what has remained markedly less clear is the fact that Fury is the most important singer in the history of post-war British pop music – and if I were to extend the field to include pre-war singers, Al Bowlly might be his only rival.

The reasons for this are fairly simple to outline; Fury was a singer with the rare ability to convey both sides of his personality at the same time – he could be simultaneously exuberant and threatening, at one space reassuring and alienating, and whichever side of him was dominant, the other side never quite crept out of vision – and even though he was always at the service of whatever song he was given to sing, he is never either comfortably mainstream or extravagantly out of bounds; he never lets you forget that you are listening to and watching him, however many pullover masks he has to don.

As far as rock and roll is concerned, Fury was also the first British rocker really to mean it; while Larry Parnes' self-assembled gallery of shy, distracted teenagers is finally not that far removed in theory or practice from Simon Cowell's ring-road-mastery, Fury immediately penetrated beyond dreams of cheerful gayness. His debut single was self-penned – an extreme rarity in fifties Britpop – and all of his package tour colleagues, from Vince Eager to Jimmy Tarbuck, were taken aback by the mere presence of a guitar, let alone his writing of songs on it. There was the early Cliff, of course, but he was quick to exchange hip swivels for Lionel Bart singalongs as soon as his chart positions diminished, and his permanence is more the result of astute reading of the demographic weather; he has changed slowly and imperceptively but always decisively and is sufficiently astute to lob out the odd curveball – a "We Don't Talk Anymore," a "Some People," a "What Car?" – in order to demonstrate that he's still in the loop.

And the rock and roll, finally, never left Fury; *The Sound Of Fury* deserves its reputation as the first recognizable British rock album, and even when charting with tremulous, hugely orchestrated ballads later in the sixties he was still cutting sensuous, elongated readings of things like Jimmy Reed's "Baby What You Want Me To Do?" – which brings me to Fury's decisive X factor; he was the first British pop singer in the rock and roll era to introduce sex into our bloodstream. Listen to his highly sated sighs of ecstasy punctuating the wide open spaces of 1960's "Wondrous Place" or, most sublimely, the irreducible and unwriteable plea-turning-to-growl on 1963's "Like I've Never Been Gone," whence he turns the "you" of his anxious "guilty for loving you" into a multisyllabic but wordless descent from humility to seduction. Was any other British singer of the period capable of such emotional or spiritual/carnal shifts – the preppy politesse of sundry Bobbys subverted into real blood and fluid? It's little wonder that the Silver Beatles rushed to apply for the job of Fury's backing band (though finally declined after Fury's insistence that they get rid of duff bass player Stuart Sutcliffe) and that others included the nascent Blue Flames (with another Parnes protégé, Georgie Fame, on keyboards) and the Tornados.

Fury was quick to rise above his contemporaries, and the baffling absence of any number one singles in his chart record (though his energization of "Halfway To Paradise" topped the

NME lists) suggests a silent rebuke for not fully playing the game, for not indulging in cuddly hiccups like Adam Faith (whose chirpy run of hits always seemed to me like a test run for the more fulfilling careers of actor and City financier, not to mention an important training ground for his arranger John Barry) or fitting all sizes like Cliff effortlessly managed. Fury seemed too real for this all-round circus of wannabe family entertainment (though conversely this was also the age when getting married could kill your career stone dead, as happened with Marty Wilde – the attendant irony of his family helping to make him one of the least expected architects of New Pop a generation later need scarcely be underlined). The strangely familiar quiff and gold lamé jacket he sports in the film *Play It Cool* of course spell 1982 in retrospect – hello, Martin Fry – but also induces no small regret that Fury didn't have a greater say over where his career was going; unhappy appearances in panto and TV variety shows confirmed a world which simply was not his, and certainly (to paraphrase the late Richard Cook) if Fury had been twenty years younger and starting up in the age of New Pop he would have been a figure equivalent to a Fry or a Weller or an O'Dowd, an icon of his own making (to think of what he might have accomplished with, say, Trevor Horn had he survived longer is heartbreaking to contemplate).

That having been said, he became a sturdily noble but quietly subversive balladeer, and his inescapable reality and appeal saw him well through the Beat Boom; he was still racking up hits as late as 1966 and still experimenting – his single "Don't Let A Little Pride (Stand In Your Way)" from that year remarkably finds him absorbing ska and bluebeat. But finally the times overtook him; he switched from Decca to EMI to release an extraordinary sequence of singles, many of which absorbed psychedelia, and it remains a matter of regret that these have still not been satisfactorily compiled.

None of them made the charts, however, and his health was

also beginning to suffer; several childhood attacks of rheumatic fever had rendered his heart extremely vulnerable and he was certainly more than aware of his potentially limited lifespan. This made his unexpected re-emergence as the fictitious Stormy Tempest (though many say based on real-life Merseybeat foot soldier Rory Storm) in 1973's film *That'll Be The Day* all the more astonishing; he does not appear for long, but every appearance is like a butterfly exploding into a colossus – he is so unquestionably real that he nearly embarrasses the rest of the film into exposure as a fancy dress party (and it is a superb film with fine and truthful performances by everyone from David Essex to ex-Rory Storm and the Hurricanes sideman Ringo Starr).

The opportunity for him to prosper again was very clearly marked. But he didn't, or couldn't, follow it through; there were further heart scares and surgery and he eventually settled for a quiet life in the country, breeding horses and sheep and becoming active on the conservation front. However, in 1981 there came the real chance of a musical comeback; Stuart Colman, producer and mastermind behind the belated success of Shakin' Stevens, persuaded him back into the studio, and in 1982 his name began to reappear in the lower regions of the charts. He did a few well-received concerts, participated in the Channel 4 nostalgia series *Unforgettable* (again with such natural power, even in diminished health) – but it finally proved too much and suddenly he was gone, the same age as Elvis.

"Run To My Loving Arms" was one of the melodramatic ballads in which Fury tended to specialize towards the end of his initial chart run; it comes from 1965 and wasn't an especially big hit, but for its time it still sounds remarkably contemporary, with Ivor Raymonde's expansive arrangement easily joining the dots with Dusty and the Walkers. What distinguished Fury as a ballad singer was a kind of not-quite-ruined dignity; in songs like "I'm Lost Without You" ("You're My World" in negative, down to the repeated bassoon figure) he does not seek to impress his immense internal grief upon the listener but merely sings of it, as best he can, without melismatic fireworks. He is down but never ever quite out, and thus able to assert the slightly desperate reassurance of "Run To My Loving Arms" – slightly desperate because he elides over phrases like "filled with tears" as though his own eyes are raining, and yet he is singing of his wish to shield and comfort his would-be Other. Somehow he manages it – Frankie Laine is not often cited as a comparison but Fury certainly deploys some of Laine's tendencies here; the rolling-verging-on-shrill vibrato in the choruses, again the Victor Mature-type tower of strength liable to be knocked over by the littlest of fingers. And Fury inhabits the song as though determined to prove that he is for real – the extended question mark pause of high unison violins which follows "They'll take you in and make things right" (as if to enquire "are you really strong enough to see this through?"). But Fury finally rides his steed of hope; note how in the final chorus the tympani and drums double up as he approaches her more and more closely, how the bass suddenly brightens into octave-leaping bounds, and – finally and purely – his final "arms" which come down in four stages as he bends to embrace her, such that the abrupt mid-song ending does not feel like losing one's toehold astride the Grand Canyon (unlike, for example, Kenny Carter's "Showdown") but more like a happy ending, a consolidation, a bridge built. It was one of the few happy endings he was to receive. But who would now be big and small enough to want to be Billy Fury?

35

Michael Crawford: The Music Of The Night

19 February 2008

According to the flattened-out picture, 1987 was a year of laminated gloss, of smoothed-out roughness, of voices impersonating soulful in airtight soul-excluding canisters; the year purely and far from simply of Pernod adverts, the Real Musician playing the saxophone on Waterloo Bridge in that Kronenberg 1669 commercial, the era of assumed prosperity about to be routed by Black Monday. "Down To Earth"? Curiosity Killed The Cat (there's the central warning in itself) do everything they can to nullify any sense of true roots, leaving an unplaced, affable-meaning glide of sourceless airsmoke, so seamless that there's no risk of any razor's edge upon which Ben might impale his beret. Even more markedly, a 1987 church which could accommodate both Chicago House and *The Phantom Of The Opera* had to be a broad one. Certainly for today's purposes "The Music Of The Night" may count as this Top 20's strangest and least in place entry.

Forget for a moment the musical itself, and maybe even the story, since in the show the Phantom lures the would-be heroine Christine to his hideaway, seducing her with his unknown airs (i.e. the song under consideration) until at the point of climax he pulls the curtain away to reveal a minutely-detailed, life-sized replica doll of the now terrified woman. The plot can be guessed; this can't be a Rochester since his wooing is active rather than unknowingly passive (Jane has to wait for Rochester to "see" what she's offering him) and he has ulterior motives; when at the show's climax he pleads with Christine to see beyond his face, she responds that she is afraid of his soul rather than his looks. For these purposes I am more interested in this song as a record in itself, and in particular Michael Crawford's reading of it. It has been said that Crawford had no formal musical training before accepting the role of Phantom, although he had gamely appeared, nearly a quarter of a century earlier, alongside Streisand in the movie of *Hello Dolly!* Certainly his tenor wavers and quavers at key points in "The Music Of The Night" but the instability of technique matches that of his character's mind – and, more pressingly, that of the character for which he had previously been best known.

If we take "The Music Of The Night" as signifying mock-sinister, finally unraveling to reveal a tender and rather afraid and vulnerable man barred from the world through no fault of his own, then it is difficult from a British fortysomething perspective not to think of Frank Spencer. Since Asperger's syndrome was not formally diagnosed until 1981, I cannot think of *Some Mothers Do 'Ave 'Em* being constructed with that knowing a perspective; both Crawford and writer Raymond Allen have stated that Spencer was simply a domesticated update of Stan Laurel. When viewing the series, however, a disturbing dichotomy becomes apparent; here is someone who in close up is unable to understand or execute the simplest of tasks, and yet when in dire trouble (with all those outdoor setpieces) he is extraordinarily nimble and athletic, timing his pratfalls, jumps and landings perfectly. It is as though he can only truly become himself when situations rise to a near uncontrollable pitch. He can come straight off a skating line, break through a brick wall and jump onto a passing truck in ways balletic – but ask him to mend a fuse or change a light bulb and chaos ensues for everyone and everything else.

Thus I think of "The Music Of The Night" as sung by a self-reforming Frank Spencer, and Charles Hart's functional lyric allows plenty of space for Crawford to act all of his entreaties –

"grasp it, sense it," "hear it, feel it" – and sometimes he sounds like a vaguely threatening phantom but this is balanced out by moments which are utterly Spencerian (the first "darkness" in "darkness stirs" for example). Yet as Frank he sounds awed at these new powers which he has found within himself, as though he too will see the Queen on Christmas Day, and in the song's high C climax – which he attains comfortably, with or without the aid of varispeeding – one can hear the Spencer and the Phantom fighting for control of Crawford's mind and body; that "set you **FREE!**" is a cry of liberation from the unfeeling bureaucrats who just didn't get Frank, even after he'd accidentally demolished/flooded/burned down their houses/offices.

But the song is also a subtle commentary on the dominion which music can claim on the semi-wary passive receptor of a listener; the senses succumbing to the hints and suggestions, the pleas, the invitations – in this sense it is a reply to Helen Reddy's "Angie Baby" where the girl finally gets swallowed by her radio. "The Music Of The Night" is the swallower's serenade.

Or perhaps just up to a point. "Touch me, trust me" he pleas in the final verse – and we are immediately reminded of Lloyd Webber's lyricists and their instinctive cynicism towards unquestioning belief and worship, whether Christ, Eva or Norma Desmond. But just as quickly it becomes clear that this man may not quite know how to love himself – at the end of the song he quietens and finally opens himself up, discarding the mask to reveal Frank, always ahead of Ben in the iconic beret sense – in the final word, even, that last "night" which settles against a slowly raising eyebrow slow string flourish which bravely finishes on an unresolved atonality. "You alone can make my song take flight" – and here is the still silent Rochester, regardless of what goes on to happen in The Phantom Of The Opera proper.

36

Glenn Gould/Bach: Fugue For Keyboard No 20 in A Minor (BWV 865)

22 February 2008

Thinking about Teo Macero, who has just died – the original cut-and-paste man, jazz's own Burroughs – I wonder how influenced he was by Gould. Certainly he was under the spell of Mingus, in whose Jazz Workshop he served throughout the first half of the fifties, and then, after Mingus and producer Bob Thiele had devised the notion of overdubs and tape splices to enhance 1963's *Black Saint And The Sinner Lady*, Macero then proceeded to his monumental body of never-performed work with Miles; a tapestry from *In A Silent Way* to *Get Up With It*, an exhibition of "spontaneous" performances which never actually took place; long improvisational wanderings edited down, phased, tweaked, cut up, rolled over and made to work as discrete records, and it is little wonder that they sounded like music not of this planet.

But, as I said, there was also Gould; the vacillating artist who could never find it in himself to trust live, or "real" performances. His series of radio soundscapes for CBC – the word "documentary" manifestly fails to do them justice – are processed, sculpted meditations, contrived to fit, but never are their contents untrue or dishonest; artistically they are magical, emotionally and logically they are revelatory and illuminating.

His complete recordings of the two books of Bach's *Well-Tempered Clavier* took eight fitful years to record, from 1963 to 1971. His reading (and I use the singular case advisedly) of what Gould called "the celebrated obstacle course," the titanic A

Minor Fugue, is actually spliced together from two separate takes. Though both were note-perfect and in the same tempo, the emotions attached to them were very different; one take Gould deemed too mournful, too machine-like, too Teutonic, and the other he thought far too happy and bright for the material under consideration. After some consultation, excerpts from both takes were cut and spliced together to make a satisfactory whole.

The editing is expertly done; the shifts occur every 30 seconds or so, but only extremely close listening will reveal the joins. The "performance" hence becomes simultaneously jubilant and pining, at one time efficiently robotic and fervently human, thus providing us with a thought-through glimpse of the two minds which Gould was wont to house. Like life, it goes up and down and back again, though resolves considerably more tidily; and while one can see the point of Gould's reference to the "Dixieland beat" undertow of the B Minor Fugue which concludes Book I, since he evidently prefers its jaunty splashes to the stricter post-Webern pointillism at which he was striving. It is rather like listening to a man who can't make up his mind whether to laugh or cry, but is in the end glad to do both at once. The imperfections emphasize his willfully messy and merrily wild perfection, and finally it doesn't matter whether or not this was ever really "played" since it plays both with and into the mind of the listener - and the emotional rewards are no less vast.

37

Ray Noble and the New Mayfair Novelty Orchestra with vocal refrain by Al Bowlly: Twentieth Century Blues

20 March 2008

It begins with the rainfall rumble of two pianos – played by Ray Noble and Harry Jacobson – with sweetness gradually being subsumed by whole tone discordancy, symbolizing the perceived replacement of old and gracious with new and crass. Then Max Goldberg's plunger-muted trumpet growls out a lugubrious ex-working man's blues, succeeded by a hopeful comfort blanket of low-register clarinet. It is November 1931, just over four months since my father's birth, and the prelude to the Great Depression. Affairs are far from happy.

Then HE enters – with an extended moan of "Blues" which is simultaneously vast and intimate, angered but cordial. He sings Coward's lament of drear and din, chaos and confusion, and sounds only a little more assured than Coward that it is the times which have gone wrong, rather than himself. "What is there to strive for, love or keep alive for?" he asks, and only half knowing that he is part of the answer (as opposed to Lydon two or three generations later, who possessed full knowledge that he was forming the future when he snorted "No future").It would not really be truthful to say that prior to Al Bowlly, there was no such thing as the English popular singing voice, but the dividing line had been sternly firm – the costermonger's yellow yells and mangled labials of the reckless music hall tradition, barked without need of megaphone or metaphor, directed directly at its intended audience; or the politesse of the post-

Victorian parlor recital with plums for vowels, vibrati as shaky but steadfast as Stephenson's Rocket – Donald Peers' surprise 1968-9 smash "Please Don't Go" was perhaps the last audible gasp of the latter tradition in the public market.

But Bowlly came from somewhere else, so no wonder that he made a difference. Of mixed Greek/Lebanese parentage, he grew up in South Africa and methodically worked his way over to Britain as a singer and guitarist. And it is with Bowlly that the remarkable mainstream of British popular singing, for workable purposes, really starts. There were both sensuality and threat in his tones (and Dennis Potter was quick to pick up and magnify both tendencies), a rumbling assurance derived in part from Armstrong and a closeness modified from Crosby (for instance, the italicized triplicate of "Say, hey hey, call it a day" in "Twentieth Century Blues"); relaxed but menacing, almost akin to an undue ejaculation within earshot of Lord Reith, with an innocent grin to meet the sternly swerving head.

Even when the "refrain" part of the song has ended, Bowlly, like Elvis in '69 Memphis, can't let go of either song or feeling; his "Blues, blues, blues" murmur, every "blues" half a second longer and half a tone lower than the previous one, is like a rake descending into his basement, luxuriating in the low light; trumpet and clarinet lead one last perky attempt at reconciliation with those then current times by doubling the tempo before gloomily descending into the elegiac and the pissed off, even if Bowlly determined to be above, if not beyond, the latter. "Why is it that civilized humanity can make this world so wrong?" – are we really that far from "Oh, mercy mercy me, things ain't what they . . .USED to be"? The times were certainly dread-filled enough to make both Coward and Bowlly want to holler.

38

Donna Summer: This Time I Know It's For Real

25 March 2008

Almost the nineties, on the threshold of the decade which she and Moroder helped invent, and Donna Summer couldn't get arrested; the alleged comments on AIDS victims had torpedoed her career in the latter half of the eighties with only scant photocopies of hit records (e.g. 1987's burningly strange "Dinner With Gershwin") and the defiant Bronski Beat/Marc Almond reshaping of "I Feel Love" had outsold most of her eighties work put together.

At the other end of this particular telescope, it was Germany in the early seventies, and a young A&R man named Pete Waterman had approached Summer with a view to her joining the German dance act Silver Convention. But Summer went with Giorgio instead, and Silver Convention's own brief but buoyant run of international hits ("Fly Robin Fly," "Get Up And Boogie") went on to demonstrate that sometimes common language reached beyond barriers of words.

But in 1989, Stock Aitken & Waterman brought her back for one last Hail Mary of disco poignancy. The huge drone at the beginning of "This Time" stands like a particularly querulous question mark before A Linn's trademark jacks trot into the picture. The record's reflectively golden melancholy is helped by SAW's early adoption of Detroit techno mores, including Kevin Saunderson's patented synth-as-tuned-drums patterns; but there is also a briskness which signifies that we must continue to move on.

Donna Summer. She loves him but whatever she tries she can't get him to notice - walk a tightrope, write his name across the sky, shout through a megaphone, get on the radio, on the TV news, lease out a skyscraping neon sign – but she continues to strive in the full knowledge that he will end up unable to help noticing her and responding, with elegant chord changes which in another world could have come straight out of Gershwin (the deceptively complex musical world of SAW, indeed).Then the chorus, and her voice is sufficient to rip through any skies, yearning, proclaiming (her growl on the "hands" of "when I get my hands on you" is the anti-Bros antidote), refusing to resign, fireworking the heavens with the neon Bible of the song's title, relaxing in the instrumental break with her offhand "oh, baby"s to counterbalance the nearly unbearable tension band wiring of "If I wait for you too long I might EXPLODE!"

On her last, climactic "real," the breath of which she will hold forever until he comes to love her, the express train of the music continues in a cautiously celebratory but also rather sad manner; those implied minor keys, but the possibility of failure or ignorance cannot be countenanced. They've brought her back for real, and this superlative single takes me directly back to jacking down Cromwell Road in the springy sun, the burnished ambers of Pimlico apartment blocks, visions of gold far from expired. A record of this emotional quality could not have been made without the human intensity SAW have so often been denied, just as it's easy to dismiss Jason Donovan as a Fairlight-assisted robot before recalling that "Nothing Can Divide Us" covers, in its own jolly, unsensational way, some three-and-a-half octaves.

39

Alma Cogan: If Love Were All

I April 2008

The novel which the late Gordon Burn named after the singer is as dully sober as one might expect – and that is not necessarily a pejorative, at least not until he ventures into misguided *Tales From The Crypt* territory. I am skeptical whether the real Alma would have settled for quiet, bitter retirement, since none of her fellow travelers in that remote pre-rock British pop universe seemed inclined towards it; on the contrary, most were obliged to continue struggling (relatively speaking) after rock had overnight rendered them redundant, and few of those stars seemed able to adapt – Ruby Murray, who at one point was popular enough to have five titles in the Top 20 in the same week, died in her early sixties, a forgotten alcoholic; David Whitfield, Britain's first reality show star (he came to prominence after winning *Opportunity Knocks*, then still on Radio Luxembourg), finally threw in the towel and headed for Australia, only to be felled by a fatal heart attack a couple of years afterwards; Dickie Valentine, Britain's highest paid male entertainer of the fifties and a sort of Jason to Alma's Kylie, was like many of his peers forced to downsize to the cabaret/social club circuit, and, tired out, was obliged to drive himself from engagement to engagement in a tight schedule, leading to the fatal 150 mph crash in Wales in the spring of 1971. Only those astute and flexible enough to change career went on to prosper; Dave King turned into a highly-respected actor, while Jimmy Young defied all logic with his far more profitable forty-year career as a radio broadcaster and political interviewer.

Like Kylie, Alma was bubbly, forever smiling, always a trouper (though Burn's book suggests several potential Michael Hutchence figures in her life), sought to expand her musical horizons against the wish of her paymasters and contracted cancer. Unlike Kylie, she did not survive and died in 1966 aged just 34. EMI had let go of her early the previous year – her chart career did not extend into the sixties – suspicious about such ventures as an album of big band Beatles covers (Lennon may have been a Hutchence figure himself) or working with such unlikely MoR figures as Joe Meek and Andrew Loog Oldham. In any case, she did not live long enough to develop any of these new liaisons properly, and I suspect it is our loss as much as hers.

Her "If Love Were All" was recorded in 1962, so we must dismiss any notion of a last will and testament about her performance. Yet it stands as the central island of her smilingly anguished sense of isolation – she was undoubtedly keen to embrace the new world as far as it would allow her. Noel Coward himself considered it the best version of the song that anyone had sung, including Judy Garland, and even though Cogan omits the first two verses from the introduction (those which begin, respectively, "Fate may often treat me meanly" and "Though I never really grumble").

Her version, in fact, begins with a huge sweep of operatic tragedy flourishes from the orchestra, as though Tosca has already toppled from his tower, before the waves recede and the music reduces to a single accordion, against which – out of the darkness – Cogan begins to sing: "I believe . . . in doing what I can." Her voice is not technically precise; she is striving but cannot quite reach the right scales. But she is clearly struggling, though at this point still smiling, as evidenced by her throwaway "hey ho".

The musical textures gradually thicken as she slowly unravels her essential loneliness – she falters movingly on "I think if only" but recovers, trying to giggle the line "someone affectionate and dear". Still, there is major doubt, and her naked fear is only partially concealed by courtesy as she utters the self-death sentence "But I believe that since my life began/The most I've had is just a talent to amuse," and she hangs onto her second "hey ho" with rather less assurance before the orchestra seeps back into the picture, trying to elevate her hopes by moving up a key. Yet if anything this encourages her to bring her hidden emotions out into the open; now she is barely preventing herself from breaking down with this "I think if only"; the "someone affectionate and dear" sees her bracing herself for the giant leap into only she knows what.

And with the final "talent to amuse" she loses any hope of hope; she shrivels into her own fears with the closing trio of "hey ho"s before she shakily sustains the last "all" – which is quickly faded into the ambience of the receding orchestra, cutting her off from civilization, leaving her marooned, suppressed, eventually neglected or misreported, like a girl you remember seeing passing you in a fairground forty years ago but can't quite place her being or relevance.

40

Jose Afonso: Grândola Vila Morena

I May 2008

As the field recordings sampled on Charlie Haden's original *Liberation Music Orchestra* album proved, if emotion and purpose are expressed sufficiently strongly then both will be felt regardless of the listener's knowledge of the language in which they are being expressed – and this extends to all of Tropicalia from 1968 onward, from the reactionary audience booing Caetano Veloso offstage for going electric to the mellow bitterness of Tom Jobim's *Matita Pere*, the most extreme balancing case of sweet music and enraged lyrics in all of pop.

I knew a fair bit about Zeca Afonso's life – Portugal's Guthrie, Dylan and Jara in one; committed revolutionary, a central player in the overthrow of the Salazar dictatorship who did his time, both within Portugal (in prison) and outside Portugal (in exile but still fighting for the righteous cause, and died in 1988, not quite sixty, from complications arising from Lou Gehrig's disease (thus was he also the Portuguese Mingus) – but little about his music other than knowing this song from the version performed by Haden's LMO on their 1982 album *The Ballad Of The Fallen*. Regular *BiA* reader Nuno has very kindly sent me copies of two of his key albums and I am enormously grateful for both, since Zeca's records are currently next to unobtainable in any format in Britain.

Of these, 1971's *Cantigas do Maio* seems to me his clear master-piece; a blueprint for revolution, both politically and musically. Despite my lack of understanding of the Portuguese language Zeca's voice – Seeger sturdiness meets Jobim smoothness –

transmits his feelings with more than sufficient power. Although the record is not exclusively political, the tang of the radical is palpable throughout all nine tracks – the berimbau-directed bounce of "Ronda dos Mafarricas," the percussion-only delivery of the Gal Costa hit "Milho Verde," the seamless transition from flute/acoustic fluidity to hard trumpet/electric bass edge throughout "Maio Maduro Maio," the devastated (and proto-Bon Iver) howl which blows acridly through "Cantar Alentejano," the subtle post-psychedelic effects throughout the record as a whole, and the climactic "Coro da Primavera" which alternates between a slippery groove which puts me in strange mind of the Mayer/Harriott Indo-Jazz Fusions records and defiant, free-tempo but slow motion choral anthemising.

But "Grândola Vila Morena" is for voices and massed marching feet only; celebrating the spirit of brotherhood and collaboration in the titular town, its procession is proud with no wish for turning. In April 1974 this recording was played on Portuguese radio as a signal for what would be termed the "Carnation Revolution" to begin, which shortly led to the deposing of the Salazar regime with roughly equal amounts of consequent freedom and problems. Zeca's immortality was assured, and although its humble dignity does not immediately mark it out as a revolutionary anthem, its quiet determination was instrumental in helping reshape this damaged society. An orchestra of music which helped liberate, the banner of the newly risen, and the most fitting of songs to celebrate on this May Day.

Orson Welles and the Mercury Theater: War Of The Worlds

2 June 2008

A song? Music, even? Yes, and I don't mean Ramón Raquello and Bobby Millette or any of the configurations into which Bernard Herrmann managed to corral the CBS studio orchestra – though note how, as the events become steadily clearer, the music gradually and subtly slows down from lively to mid-tempo to a solitary piano. Nor do I particularly mean the famous first half of the broadcast, the one which ensured that a lot of listeners didn't hang around to catch the second half; the initial, half-bluff, half-blind complacency of Professor Pierson ("Why must I always be challenged on these matters?" was a frequent rebuff used by Welles towards his recalcitrant actors in later times), the increasingly scrambled attempts to pretend that business is as normal and the dreadful rapidity of the horror with microphone cutouts, charred reporters' bodies, fifty feet, services in the cathedral, this is the end and the radio ham trying to locate a Mayday. We know about Welles' complete familiarity with and inbuilt suspicion of the power of the media to distort and frighten, we can probably guess that he timed the urgency of the bulletins to coincide with the moment when impatient Charlie McCarthy fans would do a radio channel scan as soon as Nelson Eddy came on to do his song, we know about the panic that arose and the absence of real casualties but also the career-building controversy, and maybe of the approaching horror of 1938/9 in general.

But hardly anyone knows that second half, after the forlorn

"2X2L"s and the Styx-bound ship foghorns, and after the CBS announcement of a commercial break, except those astute enough to know a Welles con when they heard it, or those who quickly flipped back through the dial to be reassured by the utterly unscathed tones of Edgar Bergen and Don Ameche – and although the broadcast has survived, nobody talks of that second half hour.

The sequence largely consists of a monologue, narrated by Professor Pierson, who against all odds has survived the Martian onslaught – savor that quiet but terrible joy in Welles' grave voice at the prospect of Orson Welles being the last, or only, man on Earth – and wanders away from Grover's Mill, eventually coming through Newark, after several days of walking and Martian-avoiding, and finally arriving in New York. In Newark his meditation is interrupted by the Artilleryman who crouches in doorway with knife, already half-mad, slavering over the prospect of rebuilding humanity with a view to fascism. He makes his excuses ("Where are you going?" "Not to your world ... goodbye, stranger ...") and proceeds to New York. The story turns out as the original novel does.

What I find compelling, however, is not so much the story but the way in which Welles is telling it. His voice gently – and with symphonic symmetry (his discourse is structured almost exactly as an *adagio*) – unleashes a hypnosis every bit as potent as the Martians' black smoke; it is tempting almost to forget the invasion and focus on his solitary psychogeographic proce-dural, attempting to make sense of what he now sees as measured against what he once recognized – "buildings strangely dwarfed and leveled off, as if a giant hand sliced off its highest towers with a capricious sweep of his hand." Sometimes I have to pinch myself to remember that he's not reminiscing about Glasgow circa 1980. In the end he skirts the wild dogs with their strange mouthfuls of brown meat, finds the Martians dead in Central Park and, in tandem with the incongruence of the narrative's timespan – like the protagonists of Chesterton's *The Man Who Was Thursday*, Pierson is apt to travel huge distances in practically no time – we get the impression of Pierson, falling asleep under his Princeton telescope, waking up, seeing the trees, the people, and it's all been a dream, a dream of obliteration, a warning or a desire. But surely not a prophecy; just a redder disc floating in a bluer sea?

42

No-Man: Days In The Trees

23 June 2008

Nearly twenty years old, and more or less impossible to find now – so do I leave it alone, as forlorn as the weeds and broken bricks over which it sings, or do I bring it out into the open as the song itself is so reluctant to do, since I would be hard put to put it out of my personal top ten of singles?

No-Man, but not no wonder; they continue to this day, forging a path which causes even them to lose their way now and then – their music unsentimental but clinging, its horizons universal yet as surely focused as the nose to the dagger – but "Days In The Trees" was their moment, and it should have been nineties pop's moment, had people not run from it bemused, or not even been able to hear it at all, even if it only shares with Duras the notion of mortality set against a love which even hate cannot define (how many more "even"s do I need here to beat the odds?).

Well, it was six minutes and twenty or so seconds long, the "Mahler" version at any rate (there is no definitive version of "Days In The Trees" any more than there was one of "Higher Than The Sun"; the progressive randomization of the concept of the pop single in those early post-House nineties continues to be willfully overlooked and not properly followed through), and there's the "Funky Drummer" beat slowed down to a wary Cotswolds canter, string synthesizer and real strings, Tim Bowness singing timidly, mouth half covered like a Cliff Richard who can't really get used to children seeing him crying, singing maybe a half-second too slowly for listeners to grasp, but there are the trees, and there she (or he?) is – hiding, darting, teasing, escaping? Whoever it is, they are running "to the shelter of the trees" while the singer stands there with the aforementioned weeds and broken bricks, pale fingers curling autumn grass . . .

. . .and then an awakening, or a strange and less than pleasant dawning – is he pursuer or pursued? Is he victim or perpetrator? – as piano traces out hugely regretful (and very French, so that should be rueful) chord changes. Then, a possible prayer; the crack in Bowness' larynx as he breathes in (and out) an awed whisper of "the real taste of God". But this taste isn't quite a divinity that the Kate Bush of side one of *Hounds Of Love* might have recognized; he's draining the heaven from the warmth of her breasts, but then he tears the seams "of my smooth and laundered clothes" and suddenly it is he (or is it a disguised "she"?) fleeing to the trees, climbing a rope ladder while trying to avoid hanging himself ("the ascent to your heaven") . . . an earthier but equally smoldering perspective on Mark Hollis' ideations of deliverance.

But it's when Bowness' vocal ends that the song's spirit breaks through like a Wessex Poseidon (but where's the sea? Inside one's self?) as Ben Coleman's violins take over with the apposite Mahlerian tragic flair; his melody multiplying itself as feedback and ascending "A Day In The Life" eruptions force him to become a Penderecki section – he peaks and then the music dives back into the sofa of blade-strewn grass as Coleman does some Grappelli riffing with Nyman downturns, allowing for the brief resurgence of Bowness' heaven sent ascent (but is it assent?) before the song "ends", the sky darkens, the birds, the owls, a tolling buoy of a bell, and in among the sea which has suddenly arisen out of the forest (if it ever existed), the steely icicles of the opening strings to Walker's "Such A Small Love". Hear it in tandem with the far briefer "Reich" version – the verse melody topline played on Aphex-anticipating mock-marimba while a phantom voice from *Twin Peaks* (with which this was contemporary) speaks in equal parts dread and wonder of the first time she really felt love; and sweetness just about wins out – but the resonance, the torn immaculacy, the unarticulated ghosts and truths; they all continue to refract out onto the universe, as though to prove to themselves that it is not all merely a mirror. Or is that a blue in that there air?

43

Jay-Z: Wonderwall

30 June 2008

I think you're expecting me to talk about custard pies in Noel Gallagher's face. I think you might anticipate expression of queasy joy at a "Wonderwall" worthy of the Shaggs. I think you're wanting me to speak of the scarved ringmaster, the missing link between Sammy Davis Jr and Son Of Bazerk, becalmed, energized, and his throaty BACK IN BLACK solution (the non-missing link between Bon Scott and Scott La Rock) which immediately cancelled out all 99 problems in one parceled pavement of brotherly breath. I think you'd guess that I'd consider Jay-Z the Ishmael Reed to Gallagher's Mailer (what would he do without the booze and the promise of brawl inspiration?). I think you ought to know that it's all turning wrongly right again – with ex-Skrewdriver roadies and magazine writers who thought it a pleasant idea to plaster Union Jacks on covers as an anti-American protest (the spirit of Richard Hoggart's NASTY AMERICA/THEIR LIVES ARE BETTER THAN OURS AND WE'RE SCARED BEND YOUR HEAD AND DRINK YOUR TRIANGLE OF MILK quadriceps cap lives on!) laughing at Jay-Z being at the Glasto and losing all those sales when they should have booked somebody PROPER like I don't know the FUCKING FLEET FOXES, and what the fuck, I turned on Radio 1 yesterday morning and there was a jingle from picket line disregarder Jo Whiley, still skippingly trying to pretend that a multi-millionaire company director can be down with any kids other than her own, sniggering (note the hidden word, of course) "Back in the kennel, Westwood! Glastonbury isn't just about hip hop (but it has HARDLY EVER been about hip hop)! It's about guitars because I'M SCARED because if we play you HALF A SECOND of rude rap you'll scuttle off to Virgin or Capital or xfm STAY IN YOUR BOXES LISTENERS EVEN IF WE HAVE TO NAIL THE FUCKERS DOWN because I'LL LOSE MY JOB and after all great radio is always run by fear ISN'T IT?" – just keeps on pressing because they need you to stay with your demographics (your "own kind") . . . eclectic? What is that? Eclectic Light Orchestra? That's Radio 2, isn't it? . . .

I think, therefore, you'll gather that Saturday was a glorious strawberry and absinthe lollipop of a FUCK YOU to all of that; . .and what is pop if it's not about those moments, those GLISTENING CATHODES when it all shifts into a new and better focus and you instinctively know you were rightly wrong all along? Yes, he could have done a more "purist" set (purity! authenticity! does Joe Boyd really still believe in that Indiana Jones hollow pot of bronzed truth?) and the "bitches" bother me but Civil War-old jazz slang (and probably Thoreau invented the bloody thing anyway on a ropey Wednesday afternoon just to prove a point to Ralph Waldo J Gleason Emerson) does not a Taliban make (but then: definition of a lady, someone who could walk out on stage at any time, as Beyonce could have done on Saturday, but doesn't? Where are my Ibsen Brodie's Notes when I need them?) and anyway Jay-Z's JIG-ANTIC POP-HOP was RIGHT without any capitals in the way where the Verve with their mollusc-burdened 1974-style soft rock (now is THAT not the deepest of insults to weekend audiences?) could never travel (maybe in '92 when they were still capable of quantumizing anti-solace but would you even buy a once-used Chad and Jeremy single from Ashcroft now?); the whole history lapped up in his tops and then the "FUCK BUSH!" and the extended a cappella freestyles where Doc Johnson's London (and the don Estelle), Bush fuckability and Barack BIG-ups all solidify and liquefy into a pleasing punch that everyone could lap up top and did, the solos as flighty and magnificent as prime unaccompanied Cecil T, the seemingly casual moves from references to references (rather than "songs" as such – note that back door RADICALISM of PROCESS OVER FORM, READERS) reminiscent of late-period Gil Evans or George Russell, but they were all there – Big Pimpin', and Annie, and blink and you bliss it Takeover, and Show Them Watcha Got (Jan Garbarek solitude reincorporated into a Buddy big band blast!) and Punjabi Knight Rider MC and Take Three Girls (yep) and Dirt Off Everyone's Shoulders and even as a spectator from x hundred miles away (not that many hundred, I wouldn't have thought, but huge spiritual leagues had to be negotiated on Saturday) it felt justified and less than ancient, and yes it's a fucking shame that thirty years after Kool and Flash and Bam started all this off hip hop still has to "justify" itself and boy were they waiting for the Hova to be CONTROVERSIAL and PUSHY and ABUSIVE (I contemplate the zero fuss that would have arisen if, say, Eminem had been picked to close Saturday) but no, he was as dignified and politely unapologetic as Ellington was in any given sixties festival bill his band had to be on under Christ knows who these kids are; he was unashamedly generous, humble with a genuineness that was unfakeable, but always the underlying message, THIS IS OUR MUSIC, but by being such it then becomes everyone's music, like the 200,000 at Glasto who KNEW that the old "rules" couldn't be magicked to work anymore (if they ever did, and petrified old Eavis closes the door on his future as a result of whiteboy plantation media scares), like the young black hoodies who wandered into the basement at Notting Hill MVE on Saturday afternoon and immediately undertook a detailed investigation, with much furrowed associated debate, of the basement's extensive indie section, yet another cumulatively massive rebuff to scared, old people of all ages who want us to be settled, tidy, accepting of censures and compromise – and the most important spark flying from the arc-weld of Jay-Z at Glasto on Saturday night was the one which smilingly said, there's nothing to be scared of (and the mirror on the other side to those intent to enemize: "you have EVERY-THING to fear!"). It was pop music saved, I think you'd know I was going to conclude.

44

Monchy y Alexandra: Hoja En Blanco

15 July 2008

Last Saturday I found a CD I thought I'd never see again. As usual, I stumbled across it without especially looking for it – I was literally down on my knees to assess the contents of the dusty bottom shelves of the shop – I blinked curiously at the spine, wondering where I might have seen it before, and when I pulled it out it took me a little while to work out what it was, whereupon I uttered a silent gasp.

You see, this compilation, prepared and released by Latin House DJ/lawyer John Armstrong in 1999, I had bought back then following an astonishing DJ mix set which Armstrong performed on the John Peel show. The idea of *Revolucion* was to illustrate the wide array of styles then coming to roost under the general roof of Latin House, from its origins to its future. It was and is one of the most immensely danceable of all albums, but then, as you know, things happened in 2001 and I didn't want to dance anymore and couldn't envisage ever dancing again, so I let it go. Inevitably it drifted out of print (probably was out of print by 2001) and so it became a ghost for the next seven years; something I recalled with increasing vagueness but there was also a subtly increasing urge to have and hear it again. I've no idea whether this copy I've now found is the exact same copy I sold to the exact same branch of MVE back then, but the important thing (and something that you do not get from Amazon or ebay or the chainstores) was the serendipity of finding it again now, at a time when I most assuredly am dancing again, as if it were too waiting for my ghosts to subside and settle into history.

It still sounds remarkable and hugely danceable. I note the general tone of local pride – vital when you consider the decades/centuries of shit that the Puerto Ricans have had to go through – in things like "Todo Puerto Rico" by the Bad Boy Orchestra (the same writer/producer responsible for 2 In A Room, who also appear on the compilation, a very long way from "Wiggle It"). Nuevo merengue band Fulanito are explosively brilliant, Public Enemy with accordions; their "Guallando" fulfills the fantasy of where the electro-merengue track on Duck Rock might have led.

But "Hoja En Blanco" by seemingly squeaky clean Santa Domingo boy/girl duo Monchy y Alexandra remains its most remarkable track. In his sleevenote Armstrong refers to the song as a harbinger of "bachata house" – bachata being a form of Latin song structured somewhere between bolero and blues – "a completely new style that's my tip for Latin's cutting edge this summer." The poignancy of hindsight.

It still sounds like nothing else ever, and yet like a lot of things thrown together in an Argos blender. It begins with huge, gory rave raspberries and beats as a maniacal voice yells out "grossio millennio – check it out!" Fuzzed Eno synth wobbles mixes with Nigerian hi-life guitar with the swift addition of an arsenal of live Latin percussion (always Latin House's vital heartbeat); the same maniacal voice yells in a halfway house between Rachid Taha and Joe Strummer and then the most elegant and graceful of bachata ballads (but still with the propulsive beat) makes its entry, the guitar/rhythm relations now closer to Cuba. The song plays fairly straight until the beats begin to gather gradual intensity again and suddenly (on the hinge of "hasta la LU-na!") we are back in 2 Unlimited on steroids territory, pinball whizzes, screams (especially the one at 2:29-2:30). Vintage avant-rave anti-chords ricochet at 1000 bpm while a frantic Abbott and Costello rap exchange skids into being, streaking across a nailbed of staccato consonants. Finally it's back to the central song, again sung and performed beautifully, before the rave coda adds a gasometer blink of a full stop. I'd love to think what might have happened if this had topped global charts rather than "Macarena" – but these 15 tracks are among the most vital you can listen and dance to in this age, a decade on . . . a lifetime on . . . and it's time, thankfully, to dance again.

45

The Bug: Freak Freak

21 July 2008

An idle early summer Saturday afternoon in London; time to join some more dots and try to make a greater sense of the totality. For some reason I find myself in Walthamstow and want to get back West without the increasingly dreary grind of going through "London" itself, however long it takes, but then I'm in no hurry. The 34 bus, going all the way to Barnet Church, from affable insolvency to uncaring prosperity; a timetable which optimistically gives an optimal journey time of 40 minutes. I settle in at the front, top deck, like the gawky tourist I suspect I still am after twenty-three years in this city, and we're off. Up Hoe Street, towards hard-trying suburban lanes which look better in the yellowing light; eventually proceeding towards the Crooked Billet roundabout (and the day's bookends turn out to be Crooked; several hours later, on another bus, streaking through the paceless gates of North Finchley, I pass a small, shaded and possibly shady crescent named Crooked Usage); the options are for Chingford or Edmonton, and the bus takes the North Circular westward – the parallel mirror to the A40 entrails coming in from the other side but always greyer, wider, somehow less real. When you come into London from the West the flat emptiness can be accounted for by the RAF base at Northolt (but it's all deceit; slope off at Greenford or Perivale, turn a seldom ventured corner and suddenly glimpse the city spread out beneath you like a rusty mat), but from the Eastern side the featurelessness is the feature itself. On this cut of the motorway we are bisected by two huge reservoirs, but you'd never know it from looking; instead, a forlorn mega-Sainsbury's with no apparent means of reaching there by motor or foot; assorted, isolated tower blocks daubed in hopelessly hopeful primary colored dots – is there such a thing as Tottenham at the other incline of this valley?

In the far distance, mere specks of the city; when you come out of Walthamstow Central bus station Canary Wharf blinks in your lap on the near horizon, but out here any notion of "London" is mere theory. There are glimpses of the NatWest Tower/Gherkin charged congestion; too far to touch, but it's hardly as though this is a refuge. Where do they come from, these isolated citizens at unlikely bus stops along the motorway, with no evident cluster of habitation?

Further onwards there is slender proof of a "city"; the Angel Edmonton junction, with its unappealing parades of service shops and its traffic lights which allow one car through every six minutes. Attempts at greenness as we near the North Middlesex Hospital, but this ghost is quickly given up and back into the white, horizon-free expanse. We skirt the top (or bottom?) end of Green Lanes and so far I have seen nothing to disprove the notion that this is a Sunday rather than a Saturday. To my right, unseen, Southgate, never quite engaging with my vision or conscience; and it is with some surprise that the bus abruptly arrives at Arnos Grove with its famous Art Deco Piccadilly Line station. Both Art Deco and the Piccadilly Line I kneejerkingly associate with the West, and I feel as though I've crossed a boundary, but there's little in Arnos Grove to suggest opulence (and in any case the bigger, bolder Art Deco stopoff at Park Royal is far worthier of idolatry); a scant process of shops for an age which hasn't quite been told that shops are no longer needed. Next to the tube station, a markedly enlarged car park, maybe for daytrippers wanting to take its picture (but Southgate station itself! Or Hanger Lane, even though it's on the Central Line and you have to cross twenty-seven different roads to reach there!).

After Arnos Grove, however, the land turns greener and more obviously opulent; through the dim beams of New Southgate and we're out in the sticks now right enough, the large, gobbling drives of Whetstone, Peter Sellers' old stamping ground, N20 but a fading feeling of Londonness and I'm beginning to wonder if I'll get back home for the evening. But once you get to the shops of Whetstone's whitened High Road you realize that the systematic desolation becomes increasingly subtler (as opposed to the derelict shutters which now constitute the majority of the non-tourist, Mornington Crescent end of Camden High Street); vacant or closing shops, a Waitrose which looks transposed from 1971 Blantyre, a huge and open but largely empty grocer's called DEMOS across the way, a couple of interesting looking charity shops (but interesting enough to come all this way again?).

The roads start to tend towards the vertical and swift turning, is there a London out there at all? We are now heightening up towards High Barnet, Hertfordshire, the borough of Enfield, and the traffic slows up; a herd of red shirts gives it away – it's local football passage (but in July? Out of season?). The crowd is affable but uninterested. The bus crawls patiently up the incline (and incline's the word; this is where all those GOLF SALE banners will go to retire once Westminster Council's outlawed them, banished them from the metropolis, just as the Boris-loving suburban burghers of these parts have banished socialism, fearful of that winking anti-jewel sitting in the middle of their rim called a city) and as we approach the Clochemerle walkabouts of Barnet town centre it's time to call a halt and get back. Shops shut but pubs doing brisk business.

I don't quite know (yet) what, if anything, I learned from this "day out" (nor from the journey back, which took me through the rich emptiness of Finchley and Hendon via the beaming apocalypse of Brent Cross to the foreboding bustle of Willesden and Harlesden, and even then onward, onward, a surprisingly long way onward – I didn't recall my journeys home from the Mean Fiddler back in the 1989 or 1992 day being quite as long as this – until I returned to a London that I recognized) but folded together there was – well, not quite the hint of imminent ends, not really the smell of fear (but then it was the daytime, early evening, in the summer, and sunny) but the old story of continuing, affable and irreversible decline, a system on its diplomatically dying fall. Naturally, taking the same journey at, say, two in the morning would have presented a considerably harsher story, but the question " London – what is it for?" was more prominent than any of the yawningly stretching skies I encountered.

A soundtrack to all this? Given the schoolgirls furiously freestyling to some ragga mp3 shoutouts on the 326 coming back from High Barnet towards Brent Cross (Lady Saw, I think) I'd say that *London Zoo* is in 2008 London just about unimprovable. I approached the record, as yet unheard, with some cynicism; yes, Kevin Martin, a mover and chancer who's been around as long as (or longer than) I have, ageing anti-Lothario trying to hitch a chase on the outsourcing dubstep ambulance, yes, stock *Wire* rave review, yes, tell me something I don't know already, yes, life is shit but it's not **ALL** shit, is this noise noisome enough to annoy?

All of which preconceptions shatter to bits the instant Tippa Irie storms in over Cristal-clear military two-step beats on "Angry," ranting with splendid spleen and in perfect time against the collapsing world, or at least the world collapsing in on his people – allegations of suicide bombing, the determined drowning of post-Katrina New Orleans, Tippa's even more determined double-time toasting, the dead tone which hovers in the middleground all the way through – and it sounds like pop (I am not terribly sure that *London Zoo* IS pop but at least it acknowledges its presence), direct, dichromatic and dichotomy-free. *London Zoo* is best approached as a series of Weegee (reprocessed by Marc Atkins) snapshots of the city at its various points of potential explosion; Ellroy paced, brisk, abrupt sentences, communiques from border posts, all incensed and/or confused. Flowdan from Roll Deep reports from not far from where my bus journey started, his Johnny Cash baritone solemnly spelling out all possible syllables of doom (the "nurse, hearse, black" mantras which climax "Skeng"), and from the South, Ricky Ranking, associate of Roots Manuva (whose *Run Come Save Me* is an equally stark and eloquent portrait of a declining 21st century London, seeking release via elliptical, quasi-surrealist leaps), who is cast as the Voice of Reason (even as SW9 and SW2 crumble like outdated Wagon Wheels around him); he is given the final word in the long, ominously luxurious unfolding finale of "Judgement", the warning of the madness, the vampires (Bram Stoker, Procter & Gamble, Purfleet, the Dartford Crossing, the chemical genesis of the M25, the ultimate escape from urbanization, literally a "sub" option). There is Voodoo Queen, exceptional in a way in which only someone who can remember '81-2 first hand could be; her "Insane" is like the Slits doing Gnarls Barkley – is she going crazy or is it just the world going mad? Eventually her voice constructs a self-diaspora and divides in two, again coming, or stumbling, together with a laughing, misworded and mistimed (and therefore infinitely superior) reading of "Mad World." Even the relief is for the most part superficial; on "You & Me" Roger Robinson, deceptively light of tone, plays the part of the High Barnet High Tory, interested only in protecting himself and his, even as the river sweeps the streets away into their own watery burial as the electric currents of the musical backing switch on and off with slowly increasing franticity. And, where targets need to be struck, Superape (so much more impressive and to the point here than he was on his Burial cameo, or on his own debut album) unleashes the furiously articulate "Fuckaz" wherein he bloodily damns all patronizing phonies as well as the oppressors, correctly seeing in both parties the aim to deter him and his people from bettering and improving their status in life. His intensity is unmissable, his venom justified and incendiary – though the track's most unsettling moment comes after he's ended his diatribe and is answered by a choir of unholy, stuttering ghosts as the rhythm keeps stopping and stealthily restarting; and note his constant reiterations of "Believe me!" and "Trust me!" with the roar of "LOOK AT THE STATE OF YOUR OWN HOME!!"

But "Freak Freak" is Martin on his own, the album's only instrumental and the perfect accompaniment to the carapace of expansive vacancy I viewed on Saturday, moving in and out of consciousness, touching upon glitch, dub and ambient with equal skill and purpose and perhaps this represents Martin's real coming into the light as an artist; given a contextual purpose for his anger, his sense of space has finally come into play – the radicalism is still vibrant but now we see discernible causes and even (in "Judgement") potential solutions. It's perhaps telling that while working on this record Martin was effectively living in his studio – rents were too high (the stage being prepared for a London where eventually no one will be allowed to live except celebrities, international tax dodgers and hedge fund managers, if we're talking Crooked Usage) and the project had to live and breathe, even if more easily than he could – but with *London Zoo* there is the feeling, which I haven't noticed on any of his previous records (whatever their other virtues – Techno-Animal's "Dead Man's Curve" is in its post-DJ Scud 2001 way one of the singles of the decade), that this is both something that he had to say and that he has given deep thought to how he wants to say it. Perhaps we have both had to come a long way, in our own ways, in recent years, but the expression of a crushingly oppressed culture (even if it took a white man to bring it all together – Chris McGregor's Brotherhood of Breath, never forget) is comparable to that demonstrated on something like Archie Shepp's "Portrait Of Robert Thompson" – the freeplay howls "WHY?" and the historical context ("Portrait Of A Kiss," Sousa marches, Tippa Irie) suggests *because.*

46

The Cuban Boys: Theme For Prim & Proper

28 July 2008

Almost at the other end of its decade, this number has begun to sound horribly relevant again. The Cuban Boys – who were they, really, or ever, and did it matter? Peel loved them and they came within a corporate ace of getting the century's last number one with a knowledgeable novelty hit which predated and bettered Crazy Frog. And then they released one unsatisfactory album with the unsatisfactory title of *Eastwood* – unsatisfactory for *De La Soul Is Dead*-type sample copyright clearance reasons – and vanished into the first webspace they could find in which to poke their toes.

Perhaps because of their temporary EMI connection I had it in my mind that they were really the Pet Shop Boys – I thank the reader who voiced my unspoken suspicion that the PSBs were behind "Whispering Your Name" – and "Theme For Prim & Proper", with its melancholically aggressive harmonic reminders of "Opportunities", appeared to confirm this, albeit very briefly. It only appeared as a seven-inch, on yellowing vinyl, in a run of a thousand so you had to be quick to pick it up; it is absent from *Eastwood* and the version on their MySpace page is a revised one.

Yet it seems to me their masterpiece; essentially a series of cut-ups of dialogue from the 1960 film *School for Scoundrels*, an adaptation from Stephen Potter's *Oneupmanship* series of books – an extended parody which came dangerously close to celebrating that which it intended to debunk – set to bubbling and climactically key changing electropop, it contrasts the spent politesse of Ian Carmichael's stock innocent patsy (his "I say, I'm terribly sorry" is the record's leitmotif) with Terry-Thomas' equally stock cad (how many different flavors of vile can make up the withering damnation of a term that is "hard cheese"?) and sundry voices off ("Lovely day, Henry!"). It sounds, frankly, like the Cameron and Johnson club in postgraduate conference, all sinisterly centered by Alastair Sim (as Potter)'s doomy pronouncements of the meaning and purpose of oneupmanship ("somewhere, somehow ... he has become less than you"). Interspersed are a dirty sod's "he-LLO!" (probably Terry-Thomas again) and a cry of "All his dirty rotten tricks!" from what sounds like Charles Hawtrey, but the record's climax comes in its serial closing key ascensions where Carmichael howls "Don't just stand there, Mr Potter, do something!" as he realizes that the real shit is coming to the boil. Substitute "Mr Brown" for "Mr Potter" and we can invoke that most dated of clichés, the one about this track being recorded last week.

47

Karlheinz Stockhausen/Theatre Of Voices: Stimmung (Copenhagen Version)

4 August 2008

Listening to the performance of *Stimmung* by Theatre of Voices at the Proms this Saturday just past, I almost cursed the New Seekers and Bucks Fizz for not having the gumption to do a cover version – certainly it could scarcely be further out there, or anywhere, than the former's Tommy medley or the latter's "My Camera Never Lies" – since in any version it is a deceitful lullaby; you can lie back and let the microphonic and vocal overtones and undertones feed through you, only to be jarred by a sudden surge of rasping dissonance, or the hint of a meaning above "just intonation".

I won't go through the compositional and organizational mechanics of *Stimmung* here since this should be about how Stockhausen's blue colors my air; enough to say that in the cupped cautiousness of Singcircle's mid-seventies Paris Version or the more confident and overt theatricalism of Paul Hillier's subsequent Copenhagen Version – the latter has been recorded but is still best experienced live, as it was on Saturday, with the vital room for mistakes and intuition – we can discern six people sitting in a room, around a table like the Knights or the Brontës, quite unlike the room everyone else is in now, and how their stories intermingle into one slow and subtle attestation of unattributable faith. Or you could simply view it as eighty minutes or so of long, self-phasing drones interspersed with occasional mutters of variable volume.

Certainly the Paris Version came to my teenage attention at

more or less the same time as Reich's *Music For 18 Musicians* – a comparison at which Stockhausen would instantly have bridled, since he would have argued *Stimmung* as being the natural extension of one word, or even one syllable, rather than repetitive rhythms; nonetheless, polyrhythms and repetitions provide Stimmung with its vital mechanics, though the speed is necessarily far less busy and workmanlike than Reich's. Yet its patiently unfolding meadows are a joy to absorb, not least because of the hindsight which allows us to discern the processional garbling of meaning into reverberative syllabic fascination as it would subsequently be filtered through Kraftwerk and Faust and even unto Timbaland and the Neptunes. Some of *Stimmung* is very sensual indeed, which is hardly surprising since many of its "words" are based on erotic love poetry that Stockhausen wrote for his wife in – guess the year, can't you? – 1967, and the twelve most sensitive ears on the planet may go so far as to spot the Van Morrison in Stimmung; once more, when least you're expecting it, The Word reveals itself – "Barbershop!," "Thursday!" And how could I get this far without acknowledging the unending humane drone which begins and ends *Escalator*? If *Music For 18 Musicians* exposes the industry behind making music, then *Stimmung* prolongs and emphasizes the art and for many still provides the easiest starting point for one of this past century's most remarkable aesthetic arcs.

48

Giggs: Tempa Tempa!

12 August 2008

The important thing to remember here is the cover of the CD: a park, either at dusk or dawn, the sky a strange pink, swings and roundabouts unswinging and untouched, and from this distance it looks like a stage set; above and to the left of the park, Giggs stares downwards, deep in thought. The green-on-black credits at the top read GIGGS STARRING IN: WALK IN DA PARK.

So we have to remember that the seventy or so minutes of the album are in effect a film; one grounded in some of the rawest reality you're likely to hear this or any year, but its chief architect is playing a character. How close to or far from Giggs' real life this all relates is not for me to say; suffice it to say that I wouldn't wish the life described in minute, bloody detail here upon anyone, but of course saying that already suggests a painful degree of misunderstanding.

The setting is "Peck-NAM," the war zone of nocturnal SE15, and the eighteen songs on *Walk In Da Park* more or less hang together as eighteen subdivisions of the same basic song; eighteen different perspectives on the same bleakly dark centre; throughout the album Giggs calls himself the Hollow Man (or the Blade) but his world, if it's going to end, will do so with anything but a whimper. Far removed from the nicely digestible ambient instrumentals of the second Burial album, *Walk In Da Park* is what the real drowning of South London in the credit crunch age sounds like; messy but strict, bloody but governed by its own inaccessible precepts of anti-morality.

The story Giggs tells is the one we all know (but seldom

involve our privileged selves in): a life which, as he puts it on "Who Are You To Judge?," "was all drugs, guns, girls and Master P", and which he now wants out of, or rid of. All throughout the record are tales of drug runs and drug raids, gang insults and crew decimations, an eternal night of fast car chases (at the end of the long, exacting gangster saga "Saw" his car crashes – "You're too flipping late!," "Hit the flipping brake!"), moonlit flits, loveless love (rarely has a party sounded so determinedly joyless as on "Open Up" with its brutalist Numan synth riffs, despite Giggs' midsong wink, "We're all adults, and we all love sex!") and death, death and more death.

The suite-like nature of the work is emphasized by the use of recurring leitmotifs, the "Uummm!!!" sample (possibly from Eminem and there's even a track named after it) whenever a dire crime is about to be committed, and a strange high vocal "pop" once damage has been done. But brutal, early and bloody death is the commonest recurrence; if anyone really wants to go beyond the "Disarming Britain" media facade and find out exactly what is happening in the "broken Britain" of this age and why it's happening, then go no further than Dubz' extraordinary and explicit tirade at the climax of "Pitching All Da Time" or, far more frighteningly because it's phrased so nonchalantly, the similar roll call on "Let 'Im Ave It". The police are regarded with amused contempt ("legal gang members wearing plain clothes" Giggs snarls on "Bring The Message Back", a key track where, above dismantled gospel voices and stately organ, he explains exactly why he is drawn to express "the pain and the essence"); on the fabulous "Cut Up Bag" ("UK we put cane in the cut up bag") with its soundtrack of Soft Cell after some serious cane ingestion, all slum one note synths and distinct glockenspiels – an ode to an M25 on which even Iain Sinclair wouldn't dare to venture – Giggs encourages driving listeners to wind their windows down and blast its bassline out ("No respect for the law!").

The music is some of the most exciting I've heard this year, and in British terms some of the most inventive I've heard in several years (an indicator of the recent major upsurge in quality of UK rap and grime releases: see also current albums by Skepta, Tinchy Stryder, Kano, JME, Wiley and Tinie Tempah); listen for instance to the staggering "More Maniacs" which trundles along with its synths-caught-in-a-strobe-light radiance – with Boost's deep voice intoning against descending waves of electro and the track's brisk multirhythms I am reminded of peak Simple Minds – it could be termed "New Gold Nightmare". Similarly the chaotic pile-up of "Swagga!!" sees a dozen different recordings of the William Tell Overture indulging in a tag team fight, bullets for bolero drums, rounds of machine gun fire of trumpets, and ends with a mind-altering dissolute echo/distortion reminiscent of the end of Walker's "Plastic Palace People". The operatic chorus which heralds "Click Clack!" ("Go and get your gun, we can have a dance") is set against a crushingly hard sten gun doorbell of a one-note synth riff to which are added lost soul voices, speakers from the spatial ether, universes of orchestras as well as post-drum n' bass heedlessness of rhythm. Set against this is the relatively straightforward good time anthem (as good a time as you're likely to get in Peck-Nam) "Make It Look Good" with its 78 rpm Bobby Womack samples ("Across 110th Street," aptly enough) and some sweet singing from J Melo. And, just as Giggs maintains a steady, steely baritone delivery throughout – slow motion, stealthy, assured but maybe still frozen by fear – so does the music settle down and become more contemplative as he looks for a way out; the acoustic guitar/electric piano serenity of his motherly ode of penance "You Raised Me" ("You took me to my first rave") is a good example before one final crescendo; the glitch children's choir stutters of the closing "Test Out Da Nine" where, after more personal infernos, Giggs opts to take off on a holiday, clear his mind – "I'm gonna set out to find peace" is his last testament before the heavy doors clang shut on the album (in "Bring Back The Message" he observes that "this rap thing might be my only pathway").

But "Tempa Tempa" is my favorite track of the moment, and in its matter of fact cold rationalist outlook perhaps the most quietly disturbing; over extensive samples from a song from the stage musical of *Mary Poppins* where the children are being sent down to face the judge for losing their temper ("Fuck the judge" observes Giggs dispassionately), here is London's own "Hard Knock Life"; except that here Giggs delineates the world which he inhabits in pitiless detail (cumulating in "Now your blood's floating on some fucking Red Sea shit"), all the time knowing that by doing so he's sealing his doom. I doubt we'll be hearing it on the Elaine Paige show in the near future, but *Walk In Da Park* is the starkest of documents and must be heard, although listeners would do well to remember Giggs as he appears intermittently on Westwood's show; quiet of voice and demeanor, intense of ambition, flawless in purpose.

49

Patrick Cargill: Alone On The Telephone

13 August 2008

An odd fellow, Patrick Cargill. Difficult to categorize. As with most people my age, I initially knew and recognized him as a light-footed comedy actor; he was fairly astringent in the "we're not all Rob Roys, you know" sequence of Hancock's *Blood Donor* but otherwise he was probably best known as the well meaning but bumbling star of the ITV sitcom *Father, Dear Father* (a sort of upmarket parallel to Sid James' *Bless This House*) or – for those with slightly longer memories – in the intermittent BBC2 French farce series *Ooh La La*, and it was in this persona that RCA coaxed him into the recording studio in the late summer of 1969 to record an album.

Then, slightly later in my life, I saw him playing Number 2 in the "Hammer Into Anvil" episode of *The Prisoner* and was shell-shocked. He'd already appeared as a cynical ex-colleague of McGoohan's three episodes earlier – "Many Happy Returns," that dream within a dream – but now here was cuddly Patrick of *Father, Dear Father* pressing the blade of a sword into McGoohan's forehead, slapping him around and quoting Goethe. His eyes alone could have frozen the universe. Having already driven a woman to suicide, McGoohan sets about systematically wrecking him through intimations of paranoia, and by episode's end he is a piteous, blubbering, foetal ruination of a man. I hadn't known at the time that Cargill had attended Sandhurst and served with distinction as an Army officer in India during WWII, but clearly there was a severity behind his benign façade, not that this characteristic was much exploited by writers and directors.

The involvement of RCA in the *Patrick Cargill Sings "Father, Dear Father"* album – they also bankrolled Peter Wyngarde's infamous *When Sex Leers Its Inquisitive Head* the following year – suggests a tax loss manoeuvre, but then there was a popular urge for singing actors in the wake of "Macarthur Park" and all that – even Keith Michell and Edward Woodward scored hit singles and/or albums during this period. One briefly wonders whether the likes of Colin Gordon or Kenneth Griffith were ever approached by record companies.

The Cargill album is less obviously out there than the Wyngarde one – you couldn't really get any further out than "Rape" – but it shares the notion of a concept, although Cargill's is wisely far more modest; light hearted reflections on a middle-aged man's views of the modern world, and clearly performed in character.

Well, to a point. There's light hearted, and then there's something like "Women", the nearest the album came to "Rape"-style controversy with its cheery Black and White Minstrels chorus of "Women! Women! It's a disgrace! That they are part of the human ra-a-ace!" and the track which will probably ensure that it never gets reissued on CD. Look closer, though, and the song systematically gets subverted; Cargill grumbles (essentially the whole album is 40 minutes of affable grumbling) about women drivers, women in supermarkets and restaurants, at the kitchen sink etc., is finally proved wrong and stops the song halfway with a resigned "Oh, I give up."

Cargill of course was what obituarists habitually term a "lifelong bachelor", hence the twist in "Out On A Sunday" where he turns out to be singing of his love for his vintage car and the numerous asides to his dog H.G. (there's even a track entitled "Walking With Old H.G." with offkey whistling and Cargill discussing the plot developments in chapter four of his latest novel – in *Father, Dear Father*, his character is a novelist).

Certainly there is more than a hint of gayness in his Number 2 – not least in his relationship with his assistant, the equally gay Basil Hoskins, who ends up picking a fight with McGoohan for "coming between them," lovers' tiff-style – and that in itself could lead to a useful examination of the large number of gay actors who played the nominal Village head (Eric Portman, Colin Gordon, Peter Wyngarde, Mary Morris …) but the mood of the album is decidedly camp; check out the beyond-camp "foe-dee-oh-dee-oh-doh" backing vocals in "On Art" for a start.

Despite his breezy assurances on the Free Design-ish (no, really!) "Old Man Autumn" (his equivalent of Wyngarde's "April") that "Pop is on the top" (and the rather more sinister aside in the same song of "He knows there's nothing like a fellow with a past"), he rants about modern ways very entertainingly – as a singer, Cargill is unsurprisingly proved to be a fine actor, but he had the substantial help of writer/arranger/producer Bill Shepherd (the same Bill Shepherd who oversaw *Odessa* amongst other masterpieces for the Bee Gees) though was responsible for most of the lyrics. And even then things are not quite as they seem; "Songs Of Yesterday" sees him yearning for "all the old humdingers played on Housewives' Choice" in a deliberately out-of-tune voice (but also lobs in unexpected lyrical curveballs like "consummate nerve" and "frantic benders"). "Television" is a sort of pre-emptive negation (or confirmation) of Gilbert O'Sullivan's "Nothing Rhymed" ("It's lovely to sit at home while someone is burning Rome" – also a subtle counterpart to the less than subtle rhyme on "Holiday": "Give me Roma instead of home-a").

At extremes, though, things can get rather proto-Morrisseyesque. "Nothing Is The Same Anymore" – with equally ludicrous backing vocals ("Hurrah!" "Hee hee!") – sees Cargill moaning about everything from long hair to moon landings before concluding "We're all deranged!" and signing off with an unusually bitter "I wish I was dead." Meanwhile, "Weight

Watchers Guide" has him suffer the constraints of the compelled diet ("Here's your glass of unsweetened lemon juice"), beginning with a line entirely worthy of Morrissey, "I think I'd hang for a piece of lemon meringue". His desires and cravings grow progressively bonkers throughout the song ("I'd smash any little herbert and then I'd steal his sherbet") and he ends up contemplating eating the cat with a Vincent Price-style cackle. Strangest of all, though, is "Alone On The Telephone" which starts with an enraged Cargill shrieking about being surrounded by "cretins and cranks" (definite shades of "Hammer Into Anvil" here) to a bemused parlor piano before yet another twenties vaudeville-style romp begins. He whines about the 'phone always ringing (shades of the Fun Boy Three to come?), of "helpful ideas that reduce me to tears" or "old Fred – how I wish he was dead." Halfway through the song he begins a tirade against bank managers: "Why are bank managers so interminably untrusting – and uninteresting?" and again his sanity is increasingly called into question ("Why weren't dogs given hands?"). Offers for police ball tickets are met with an impatient whistle, the jokes that his cousin tells "have peculiar smells" and finally he cracks. He's going out, and: "I'm not coming back at all. Come on H.G. – let's take a peaceful and rejuvenating walk in the park."

Hmm.

50

T.I. and Jay-Z with Kanye West and Li'l Wayne: Swagga Like Us

3 October 2008

These are the days, all right. I realize that it is virtually impossible to comprehend just how explosive and brilliant a year for music 2008 has been, even with a quarter of it left to go and the potential for even greater explosions of brilliance, from the cowering gated communities of the regurgitated PR blabbering which now passes for printed music journalism, or indeed from alleged music message boards overpopulated by the kind of people who talk to themselves at bus stops or hang around the school gates at home time. The "industry", weighed down to the point of suffocation by the fear-induced need to pander to a diminishing demographic of ageing solvent retards, would much rather you, the consumer (never the music lover, heaven forbid), stick like a cockroach to Evo-Stik to "brand loyalty", buying the wholly uncalled for fourth album by the Verve out of guilt, or those "acclaimed" Fleet Foxes or Glasvegas CDs from which you get no kicks and which you'll quietly be escorting down to the secondhand shop in six months' time, giving four stars to a two-star review of the latest Oasis album whose contents bring new meaning to the adjective "ponderous". Make do and mend. Kneel to the white elephant of the trying and overtested. As much of a twerp as David Cameron will always be, his remarks the other day about the overrated virtue of experience could be applied to the music business with infinitely more aptness.

Experience has certainly saddened me in this respect. The

startling resurgence of hip hop in 2008, the rebooting (or de-bootyfying?) of R&B, the completely unexpected second (and in my opinion greater) coming of grime – take my word for it, readers, it's like trying to sell sex to a cheese shop stuffed with eunuchs. So I merely have to shrug my shoulders and conclude that it's their loss; that the kids who routinely blast out "Swagga Like Us" on their mobiles at the back of the bus have an instinctive understanding of the magic of great pop which is de facto greater, deeper and more important than a chloroformed lecture hall full of "experts" who've heard too much to be moved by anything any more.

The opening, overiced skating rink stalagmite-dripping M.I.A. sample on "SLU" is immediate and terrifying enough to seize the listener by both lapels – a palpable starkness that places it firmly amidst the central shards of Broken 2008 Britain – that CAN'T YOU SEE WHAT'S HAPPENING desperate cry (masking a knowing grin) which the Clash kept trying to pin down (and Strummer should have lived to hear both "SLU" and "Paper Planes" – maybe the British public will do us all a favor and give these songs a one-two Frankie-style chart domination in due course). "Paper Planes" terrifies and elates in a way it took M.I.A. some time to reach and the shattering bass drones of the intro to "SLU" render its gun-toting friendship electric, particularly when the bass climbs up to meet the voice in the third loop (NO escape fucker!) and keyboards arrange themselves in equal parts Human League geometrics (the characteristic one long note followed by two double speed notes ascension, all in itself half the real tempo of the song, routinely used to build the bridges of Human League songs) and Robert Wyatt poignancy (compare curlicued notes with "Sea Song" and this).

Then the beats, those tetra-headed, eerily determined military two-step (meeting 2step) drum tattoos, a bass ample and thick enough to drown a continent in treacle, a sureness which will not entertain disputation; and then the voices, the towering babble of voices. I think of the procession of "solos" in "SLU" as an equivalent to those old Norman Granz *Jazz At The Philharmonic* jam sessions, where the greatest improvisers of their age take their choruses in succession, almost like a relay race, although of course there is a greater purpose to "SLU" than simply a jam session. It's akin to hearing Bird, Rollins, Trane and Ornette soloing, one after the other, with the "No one on the corner" acting as a kind of unifying/unison riff.

First, Kanye (who also produces), who swerves with acid beauty from naked voice to Autotune in his astounded "hundred thousand trillion" – and here is where the advancing New Pop/electro/hip hop interface solidifies into liquid; West, a visionary who's taken on Daft Punk just as Derrick May and Juan Atkins took on Depeche and Soft Cell a generation past, who has (with Weezy) rescued the Autotune from its status as a lazy tool for inadequately imperfect singers and made it work as an active and creative instrument; with West and Weezy the Autotune sounds rough, fumbling, not quite tactile, and so utterly new and exciting. "I'm Christopher Columbus, y'all just the pilgrims" he exclaims to the world; he places Mick Jagger and asthma attacks on the same aesthetic scale before his payoff: "'Cause a slave my whole life, now I'm the master!" followed by an ecstatic tongue ejection of "Naaaa-na-naaaa" as in "I won" and "McCain won't."

Then the baton is passed to the way past eek-a-boo-static Jay-Z – this track, possibly with new verses from Young Jeezy, Nas, Andre 3000 and others, is scheduled to appear on *Blueprint 3*, which promises to provide one of the abovementioned late brilliant explosions – wriggling as only he can ("Can't wear skinny jeans 'cause my nines don't fit"), dishing out fashion tips which turn Trinny and Susannah into Somerfield's specially reduced price eat by yesterday celery with a tip of the Hova hat to Art of Noise ("checkin' my fresh, checkin' checkin' my fresh"), gasping the sort of "yes" only he can gasp ("when the girls say YESSSSS...") like a space maroonee getting his first gulp of oxygen in 19 days, riding the surf of the bridge with the admirably untogether chorus of "Hoooo-vahhhh," slacking with defiant dignity.

In the third verse Li'l Weezy breaks the harmolodic barrier; swimming and swooning in his Autotuned Atlantis ("No one on the corner has swagger like MOI!"), scrambling his labials and gutturals ("Pap! No mas!" "Fo' tires!"), fascination superseding Adidas meaning, slurring his vowels like Ayler trapped in the Lyricon, and the consummating lip lick of "I know it's us 'cause we're the only thing you talk about!" before he disappears, very slowly and reluctantly, back into the chorus ("And I'm gone!" "Bye!" "Yeah!").

T.I. takes up the baton for the home strait ("Hah, you see?" "That's right" – a seamless succession to Weezy) as he ties all of the song's proud strands together ("Spin real life on hot beats") and places his newness as the logical, joyous consequence of a vibrant, active tradition ("Livin' revolutionary! Nothin' less than legendary!"). Acknowledging his "extraordinary swag" he too absorbs himself back into the song's ether, but still checking to see if you've hung on for the whole story ("OK, yeah, that's right" he responds to M.I.A.'s calls. "So you notice the song, huh?" "Tell 'em for me, Shawty!"). And so, with a final fusillade, a last machine gun run of M.I.A. swagga juice, the song echoes out, expanding to fill the entire universe.

Even in a year as fecund as 2008, T.I.'s *Paper Trail* album stands out – it's so 1982 in its own ways that it also manages to be 2022 – and everyone involved, from Rihanna and Timberlake on down, sound as though they have had no choice but to exceed themselves. The gusty "hey!"'s propelling Rihanna's jewel of an encased liberated voice on "Live Your Life" are suffi-cient to power the universe (I think of "Blow High, Blow Low" from *Oklahoma!* times 10 to the power of forever). The closing threnody of "Dead And Gone" (one of Justin's best performances to date) according to Lena – and I totally agree – occasions the application of the adjective "beautiful," a term seldom applied to hip hop. The beauty and serene swiftness of the best of 2008's music is worthy of worship and "Swagga Like Us" – a "Four Brothers" rewritten by James Baldwin for our age – forms a more than worthy temple. These *are* the days, my friends.

Contemporary culture has eliminated both the concept of the public and the figure of the intellectual. Former public spaces – both physical and cultural – are now either derelict or colonized by advertising. A cretinous anti-intellectualism presides, cheerled by expensively educated hacks in the pay of multinational corporations who reassure their bored readers that there is no need to rouse themselves from their interpassive stupor. The informal censorship internalized and propagated by the cultural workers of late capitalism generates a banal conformity that the propaganda chiefs of Stalinism could only ever have dreamt of imposing. Zer0 Books knows that another kind of discourse – intellectual without being academic, popular without being populist – is not only possible: it is already flourishing, in the regions beyond the striplit malls of so-called mass media and the neurotically bureaucratic halls of the academy. Zer0 is committed to the idea of publishing as a making public of the intellectual. It is convinced that in the unthinking, blandly consensual culture in which we live, critical and engaged theoretical reflection is more important than ever before.